MICROSOFT OFFICE 365 FOR BEGINNERS

[9 IN 1] THE ALL-IN-ONE GUIDE TO BECOME A PRO IN NO TIME (INCLUDES EXCEL, WORD, POWERPOINT, ONENOTE, ACCESS, OUTLOOK, SHAREPOINT, PUBLISHER, TEAMS, AND ONEDRIVE)

BY ADAM STEPHENS

Microsoft Office 365 for Beginners - 1st Edition

Table of Contents

Introduction

Microsoft Office 365 includes familiar applications such as Word, Excel, and PowerPoint, as well as newer apps like Microsoft Teams, Microsoft Forms, and Power Apps. Because it is cloud-based, users can access their documents and apps from any device with an internet connection, whether it's a desktop computer, laptop, tablet, or smartphone. This makes it easy to stay productive and connected no matter where you are.

We'll start by looking at Word, which is the most popular word processing program/application in the world. We'll cover everything from basic formatting to advanced features like collaboration and version control. We'll cover everything from creating basic spreadsheets to using advanced features like pivot tables and macros.

We'll also look at PowerPoint, which is used for creating presentations. We'll cover everything from creating basic slides to using advanced features like animations and slide transitions. Additionally, we'll explore Microsoft Forms, which is a survey and quiz tool that can be used to collect and analyze data. We'll cover everything from creating simple surveys to using advanced features like branching logic and question validation.

In addition to exploring these key Office 365 apps, we'll also look at some of the ways in which Office 365 can be integrated with other apps and services. Whether you're a beginner just getting started with Office 365 or an experienced user looking to learn more about the platform, this guide will provide you with the knowledge and skills you need to get the most out of Office 365.

Introduction to Microsoft Office 365

Before we begin to dive into Word, Excel and PowerPoint 365 fully, we must have in-depth knowledge about Office 365.

Office 365 which was launched in 2001, was the first cloud application of Microsoft Office and generates applications, services, and data hosted in Microsoft's servers.

Unlike the traditional Office Suite, Office 365 does not need to be installed for it to run. Also, Office 365 does not need any physical storage to store its information because it has an email hosting and a cloud storage space that allow the users to host their files online, and gain access to them, anytime and anywhere in as much they have an internet connection.

What is Microsoft Office 365

What is Office 365 Cloud Service?

Office 365 is a collection of different cloud applications which serve different purposes but similar in features. It is important to actually note that Office 365 has been synchronized as Microsoft 365 which comes with many packages such as:

- **Word:** It is a text editor specifically designed to process text, image, shapes & other features without the need to manually install it on your PC.
- **PowerPoint:** It is the software majorly constructed for presentation purposes.
- **Excel:** This is a calculation framed software used to solve the complexity of statistics, Mathematics, and plotting of graphs with other features in a flexible way.
- **Outlook:** Outlook is an email that is designed to receive incoming messages and also send outgoing messages.
- **OneDrive:** This is an online storage space specifically designed for all Microsoft users to store personal data which can be accessed anywhere around the world. It also comes with a link privilege to share files and other items stored on it.
- **OneNote:** OneNote is a note-taking software
- **To Do:** It is a task management utility that is designed to take your regular activities schedule.
- **Family Safety:** This is also another feature of Microsoft that gives the privilege to monitor your family activities such as setting screen time limits, filtering of content, activities report, and lots more to make sure family members are safe while using the internet with Microsoft.

- **Calendar:** It is used to schedule and share meetings and event times. One can automatically get reminders.
- **Skype:** This is a meeting software which is designed to make video and voice call, chat and share file or screen if need be.

Why Should I Use Office 365 over Previous Versions?

It is important to actually note that the world at large is moving fast beyond human imagination, just as we have our daily experience so also is the advancement of technology moving rapidly.

Over time, Microsoft has found it a bit difficult to release an update on the purchased version since all previous versions of Suite majorly work offline; auto-update will be difficult or impossible to occur to them all from Office 2007, Office 2010, Office 2013, Office 2016 to Office 2019. Microsoft users find it a waste of time to update since everything is working perfectly, which led to the latest version which is online-based known as Office 365. It's a cloud service that works directly from the Microsoft database for security and monitoring purposes. Very soon application installation won't relent any longer due to the rate of technology advancement daily.

Becoming a Microsoft User

Many people find it difficult to create an account with Microsoft, which without an account you can't enjoy the limitless benefits of Microsoft features. Below are steps on how to go about it:

- Go to your browser search for "Microsoft office 365", make sure it is Microsoft link then click on "Official Microsoft 365 Site - Formerly Office 365®"
- You will be brought into the Microsoft website, below is a link to "Sign in", click on it or you can also locate an image icon at your top right-hand side, you can also click on it

- Or you can directly type Microsoft website into your browser www.microsoft.com. Once the Microsoft website is done loading, look at your right-hand side you will see an image icon, click on it to create your user account
- You will be brought here, simply enter your existing Microsoft account. If you don't have one click on "Create One".
- In case you can't access your account, click on "Can't access your account" below create one, a dialog box will appear notifying you that your Windows 10 operating system will receive a security key that will give you access
- Or you want a sign-in option without you having to enter your password for reasons best known to you, simply click on "Sign-in options"
- If none of these is your case but want to create an account simply click on "Create one"
- Simply follow the instructions to get your Microsoft account opened, once done, you will be brought into Microsoft 365 environment

Benefits of using Office 365

There are tons of benefits that come with the usage of Microsoft 365, and here are a number of them;

- It has several features that make computer operations easier. Have you ever wondered how much of a good it is to copy and then paste? You don't have to worry about typing several chunks of text twice! Two buttons, and voila! You've got your result. Of course, there are many other features more sophisticated than that. But then, they are all simple and easy to execute, which is something most programmers look out for. The simpler the tasks are, the more productive users become.

- You can access your files and other details without having to carry your computer along with you. This is because your files are saved on the Microsoft cloud, and all you need to access them is a stable data connection and any of these—a mobile phone, tablet, or another computer. The very beautiful thing about this feature is that security is always tight! Without the correct password, those files can't be accessed!

- You don't have to spend time learning new features. With every system, the upgrade comes a new set of instructions and execution pathways. This can get annoying for users who are used to certain methods and routes of executing tasks. Microsoft 365 considers this as all of your old, amazing features are still installed—Microsoft Word, Microsoft Excel, and PowerPoint. The only difference is a couple of upgrades you can always get the hang of! Some other applications were added to the Microsoft 365 edition to make it even more effective. Some include Delve, SharePoint, Exchange Online, SharePoint Online, Microsoft Teams, etc.

- Microsoft 365 is an excellent choice for programmers, tech folks, and administrators. The reason is that the software was developed so that these guys have a high level of control over their activities. As mentioned above, most features are more intuitive than complex, increasing efficiency.

- After paying for your monthly rent package, you can link five different computers to the subscription. This linkage depends on the kind of plan you subscribe to, though. For companies, the number of computers that can be linked may be more. You can also activate and deactivate the license package anytime you want too. Below are some plans you can subscribe to;

Office 365 Family: With this plan, you can access these products—Word, Excel, PowerPoint, OneNote, and Outlook. This plan covers six computers and offers one terabyte of OneDrive cloud storage per connected user.

Office 365 Personal: This plan also offers access to Word, Excel, PowerPoint, OneNote, and Outlook. This one is more restricted, though. It only covers one PC or Mac, though, with one TB of OneDrive Cloud Storage.

Microsoft 365 Business Standard: This package's pricing is based on a monthly basis. The users can access Word, Excel, PowerPoint, OneNote, Outlook, and Access. Asides from that, the subscription provides services entitled to the Cloud. These services include Microsoft Teams, OneDrive, and SharePoint.

The products available on Microsoft 365 can also be accessed from your search browsers via websites. The website form of these products is grouped under the Office Online Apps—for desktops. However, Office Mobile is the platform that allows for access to mobile apps and these features, you can edit your files on your web browsers.

With Microsoft 365, users create private and public groups that allow for general communication between several groups and individuals. This way, it's easier to share ideas, and files, organize joint meetings, etc.

Microsoft 365 opens the users to features like regular backing up and upgrades of products; a ninety nine percent availability of the software tools; a pre-installed virus scanner that regularly deals with potential threats to your system, and an instant block to the upload of certain files that can be dangerous to your SharePoint environment.

Still, under the benefits of Microsoft 365, there have been several touch-ups made to the pre-existing suite, and here, we will look at a number of them.

You now have free access to Stock Images using products like Microsoft Word, PowerPoint, and Outlook. The images run into a count of about 8000 and can be found via the following procedures;

- Click the Ribbon icon at the upper right corner of the display.
- Click the command button for Pictures.
- You would then see an Insert Picture from the drop-down menu.

- Click Stock Images from the list.

P.S: The procedures above describe how the Stock Images can be accessed from Word, PowerPoint, and Excel. However, for Outlook, follow the procedures below;

- Start with the creation of a message.
- Click the panel for the email you want to work on. The panel is usually highlighted when you double-click your mouse.
- Click Insert to have a full view of the Stock Images.
- Click Insert
- Click Pictures
- Click Stock Images

There is a new array of tools and functions for Excel. One of them is the x-lookup feature. With this, you can get exactly what you're looking for on your computer at one glance. The configuration of this feature is also very easy compared to the former lookup feature. You can now create animated GIFs on PowerPoint with your slides. The amazing thing about this feature is that you can also work with black backgrounds, create intra-links to other slides, etc.

On Outlook, you can give vocal commands and messages. You can also run vocal searches without having to use highly intonated phonetics.

On Microsoft 365, everything's linked to the Web. You can fix audio clips and run through playback settings when working on your slideshows (a PowerPoint feature). For Excel, you can create and insert Intra-links to workbooks and other forms of data.

Setting up your Office 365 Account

If you want to access the wonders behind the Office 365 curtain, you would have to carry out the first step which involves creating your personal office 365 account. To start, you would have to go to www.office365.com for you to sign up. When you are on the website, the first question you will be asked by Office 365 is for you to decide if you want to use the Small Business version or if you want to use the Enterprise version of Office 365.

Microsoft designed the Enterprise version for larger organizations that can make use of lots of data and also require advanced archiving and Active Directory capabilities. Immediately you choose the Small Business, Office 365 will present you with a very simple form that you can fill it out.

You will have to provide them with your name and your Windows Live ID, you will need to sign up for windows account to get a windows ID if you don't have one already, and then you pass muster by typing the validation key and then you click OK.

The moment you click Continue, Office 365 will let you know that it is going to send your new user's name and password to the email address that you specified during the registration. The Office 365 home page will then appear, and the various services that are part of Office 365 begin to load one after the other.

Setting up a Profile

The first task, after you must have concluded in creating your Office 365 account, is to write down a little thing about you in the program—this is similar to the ones you've created on different social media sites—you would list out the basic things about who you are, where you live, and what language you are used to. Note, that the basic info about you that you made available— just like your name and address, for example—are not editable in the profile screen. That is because the Administrator that is in charge of your account is the one that is responsible for making changes to the user's accounts.

Changing Your Password

There are a few other things you are meant to do after setting up your profile and that is to set up your password. If someone created your Office 365 account for you, the person would have used a password of choice to create the account for you, and you know you need to make sure that the password is secured and no one has access to it. It means that you would need to change the password that existed before. The password you received was an autogenerated password that you'll most likely want to change whenever you log in to your Office 365 account. This is what you are to do if you want to change your password:

1. Click My Profile.
2. Click on Change Password.
3. If you are prompted, sign in again using the user's name and password; then click Close.
4. In the window for changing password, type the existing password.
5. Click in the Create New Password box, and type in a new password for your new account.
6. There is another box where you would need to type the new password a second time.
7. Then Click on Submit.

Then your password is changed to a new one.

What Makes a Good Password?

The password you are to use for your Office 365 account needs to have at least eight characters. If you want to increase the strength of the password—this will help to decrease the risk of someone being able to note your password—use a variety of uppercase and a variety of lowercase letters, numbers, and special characters. There is always a Password Strength bar that shows you how strong the password you choose is; you can now decide to make the password much stronger if you wish.

Changing Your Profile Picture

You have the opportunity to change your profile picture in Office 365 so that other people will be able to see the image you want them to see—or you can use any character, animal, or place—in various places on Office 365. If you want to change the profile picture, follow the following steps:

1. After logging in, on your profile page, click Change Photo.

2. Click on Browse, and now you would be allowed to move to the folder that contains the picture you'd like to use.
3. Select the picture, and click Open.
4. Click Upload.

Understanding the Office 365 Dashboard

The Office 365 Dashboard is the central hub for managing your Office 365 account and applications. It provides a customizable and personalized view of your account, allowing you to easily access and manage the tools you use most frequently.

When you log in to the Office 365 Dashboard, you will see a variety of tiles representing different applications and services that are available to you. These tiles are organized into different sections based on their purpose and function. Some of the common sections you may see on your Dashboard include:

1. Email and calendar: This section includes tiles for Outlook, which is the email and calendar application within Office 365.

2. Office Online: This section includes tiles for the various Office Online applications, such as Word, Excel, PowerPoint, and OneNote.

3. SharePoint: This section includes a tile for SharePoint, which is a platform for building and hosting websites, intranets, and other collaborative solutions.

4. Forms: This section includes a tile for Microsoft Forms, which is a tool for creating surveys and quizzes.

In addition to these sections, there are other sections that may be specific to your organization, such as HR resources or IT support.

The Office 365 Dashboard also provides a search bar, which allows you to search for specific applications, documents, or people within your organization. In summary, the Office 365 Dashboard is the central hub for managing your Office 365 account and applications. It provides a personalized view of your account, allowing you to easily access and manage the tools you use most frequently. By customizing your Dashboard, you can tailor your Office 365 experience to your specific needs and preferences.

An Overview of the Office 365 Apps

Microsoft 365 is a very important piece of software. The typical consumer of the subscription package will probably not make use of all of the features that are included in the package. It is important, to actually get the most out of your Microsoft 365 subscription, that you are familiar with the applications that are included in the package and available for your use. At the same time, information regarding the availability of each application within the subscriptions will be provided to assist you in selecting the appropriate subscription for your needs. Within the Microsoft 365 subscription, users have access to all of the well-known desktop applications that are part of the Microsoft Office suite. Every application consists of the following:

Microsoft Word

The word processor known as Microsoft Word may be found in the Microsoft Office 365 suite of products. Word for Windows offers support for the Portable Document Format (PDF) and OpenDocument, in addition to tools for editing and formatting documents (ODF). Word has been used as a word processing tool for a significant amount of time at this point. It is one of the company's apps that has been around the longest. Microsoft Word is actually one of the most widely used applications for writing documents since its user interface has undergone consistent development over the years, resulting in the addition of new capabilities and features. You have the option of starting over when you create new documents, or you can make use of one of the numerous pre-defined templates that are accessible. This tool may be used to produce a variety of documents, including business letters, resumes, product manuals, event flyers, and many more. In addition, you have the option of including a table of contents in your work, altering the header and footer, including colorized data tables and charts, and checking your work for spelling errors. Microsoft Word is a powerful program that may help your paper seem more polished and professional.

Microsoft Excel

The remarkable history of the spreadsheet editor known as Microsoft Excel can be traced back to its conception as a competitor to the widely used Lotus 1-2-3 spreadsheet editor and its subsequent success in outselling its predecessor. This program is a Microsoft Office app that has been around for a considerable amount of time now. It is an application for spreadsheets and a strong tool that is utilized by many people across a variety of sectors. Excel is actually used for a variety of purposes by a wide variety of people, including accountants, teachers, project managers, and company owners.

Microsoft PowerPoint

The widely used program Microsoft PowerPoint is used for the creation of slides that are used in presentations. PowerPoint is often used by lecturers and instructors to illustrate their presentations since it enables viewers to get a visual representation of the information that is being sent to them.

Additionally, business professionals use PowerPoint to keep their colleagues informed on different parts of the company, and merchants utilize it to offer a presentation to the people they serve. You will also find that the built-in templates are offered to assist you in getting a smooth start with the creation of your presentation. Your presentation may considerably educate your audience by using films, music, and animation effects, all of which are enabled by PowerPoint.

Microsoft OneNote

A tool for collecting notes, Microsoft OneNote enables you to compile handwritten or typed notes, drawings, screen grabs, and audio comments into a single area. Notes may be shared with other OneNote users via the internet or a local network using OneNote, a feature that is often underutilized or not understood at all.

Microsoft Outlook

It is designed to actually take the place of Windows Messaging, Microsoft Mail, and Schedule+. It is equipped with a calendar, an address book, a task organizer, and an email client. You may access your email account from any location in the globe by using the free web-based program known as Outlook.com, which is a web-based version of the Microsoft Outlook application.

Microsoft OneDrive

The Microsoft OneDrive service makes it possible to sync files online and then access those files from a web browser or a mobile device using the service. This is made possible by Microsoft OneDrive. The one that comes to mind first as a potential rival is Google Drive.

Microsoft Access

Microsoft Access is actually a database management system that is comprised of a comprehensive database management system formed from the combination of the relational Microsoft Jet Database Engine, a graphical user interface, and software development tools. Microsoft Access is a database management program that stores data in a format that is exclusive to the Access Jet Database Engine. Data that is saved in other applications or databases may also be imported into the application or connected directly to from inside the application itself.

Microsoft Teams

The application and service gained a lot of momentum during the COVID-19 pandemic, particularly in 2020. This was primarily because it featured one of the most useful and widely used aspects of Microsoft 365. Microsoft Teams serves as the central hub of Office 365 and is responsible for facilitating team communication, bringing members of different teams together, and providing the information and tools that are necessary for teams to be more engaged and productive. Everyone is brought closer together by the fact that they can engage at any time, whether it be by video, chat, or phone conversations. It is always possible to access documents, images, videos, the history of chat sessions, and meeting notes, which makes it much simpler to work with other individuals. The instant messaging solution that Teams provides also includes a translator, making it possible for businesses to work together regardless of the preferences and constraints they have about languages. With the help of teams, a virtual workplace can be established with all of the necessary applications, allowing workers and collaborators to remain in a single location rather than moving around from one location to another. It is frequently considered to be the workplace of the future.

Word

Introduction to Microsoft Word

It can be presumed that almost everyone uses Microsoft Word. This is because word processing tasks are so common in our lives today. A word processor can help you write letters, memos, reports, and even emails which are part of our daily lives. Word processors can go as far as editing, correcting, and rearranging text easily and quickly.

Therefore, in the chapter of this book, you'll learn the basics of Microsoft word 2022 and how to use the most important features as well as features that will help you write documents easily.

Note: Microsoft Word can be found in the Microsoft Office Suite and there are other applications in the Microsoft Suite Office, such as Microsoft Excel, Microsoft

PowerPoint, Microsoft OneNote, Microsoft Outlook, Microsoft Access, and Microsoft Publisher. However, we're only going to focus on just Microsoft Word.

The Concept of Microsoft Word

Microsoft Word is simply a word Processing Software created by Microsoft in 1983 made to help people write. It can be used on your pc, desktop, laptop, or mobile device. It is actually part of the Microsoft Office suite used by different groups, teachers, students, professionals, business owners, and people of all ages and backgrounds. It is used to make professional-looking documents, letters, reports, resumes, and so on. Another benefit of a word processor is that it makes it easy to make changes, like correcting spelling, adding, deleting, formatting, and moving text. Once the document is done, it can be printed quickly and accurately and further be saved for later changes.

Features of Microsoft Word

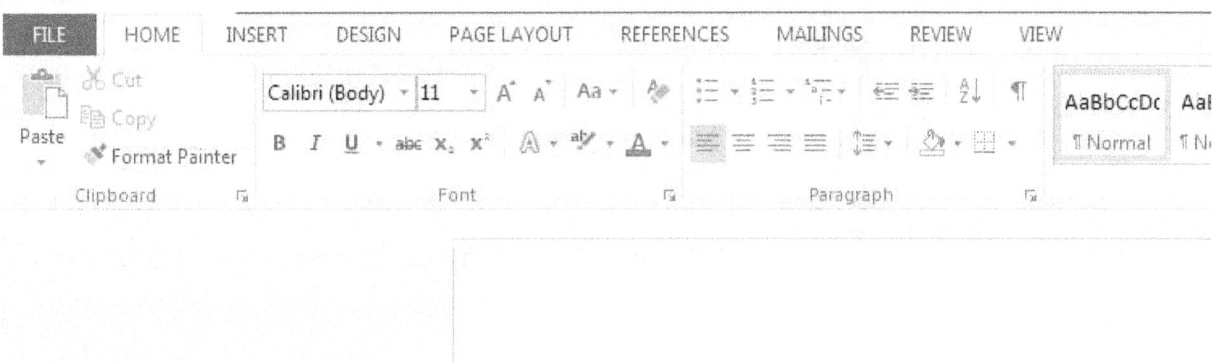

Microsoft Word has different versions from its inception. But what makes the Microsoft word 2022 version unique include;

- Simplified Word Processing - Make, manage, and even edit documents without ever having to work hard. Users from all over the world use Microsoft Word to make and share all of their documents and this current version makes it easier to achieve this.

- Rapid Document Editing - Make changes to documents with unmatched ease and speed. Correct a document's spelling, test its readability, and change its grammar with tools that are meant to make the document better.

- It lets you save any original file in a lot of different formats. .doc,.pdf,.txt,.rts,.dot,.wps, and many more formats which can be used to make documents.

- You can make beautiful and well-designed documents with no problems at all. Thanks to this great user interface! Microsoft Word has a simple interface that even the most novice computer users can use to make great documents.

Components of Microsoft Word

Now, let's talk about the components or parts of MS Word. These features let you do a lot of different things with your documents, like save, delete, style, modify, or look at the content of your documents.

1. **The File:** It has options like New, which is used to make a new document; Open (which is used to open an existing document); Save, which is used to save documents; Save As (which is used to rename a document and save it, info, options etc.

2. **The Home Tab:** In MS Word, the "Home" tab is the one that comes up when you open the program. It's usually broken down into groups: the Clipboard, Font, Style, and Editing. It lets you choose the color, font, emphasis, bullets, and where your text is. Besides that, there are also options to cut, copy, and paste in it. After selecting the home tab, you will get more options to work with.

3. **Insert:** This part can be used to input anything into your document. Examples of things you can insert are tables, words, shapes, hyperlinks, charts, signature lines, time, shapes, headers, footers, text boxes, links, boxes, equations, and so on.

4. **Draw:** Freehand drawing can be done with this tool in Ms. Word. Different types of pens for drawing are shown on this tab.

5. **Design:** Here, you can choose from documents with centred titles, off-centered headings, left-justified text and more. You can also actually choose from a variety of page borders, watermarks, and colors in the design tab.

6. **Layout:** You can use it to make your Microsoft Word documents look the way you want them to look. It has options to set margins, show line numbers, set paragraph indentation, apply themes, control page orientation and size, line breaks, and more.

7. **Review:** The Review Tab has commenting, language, translation, spell check, word count, and other tools for you to use. A good thing about it is that you can find and change comments very quickly. These options will display when you click on the review tab.

8. **Mailing:** One of the best things about Microsoft Word is that you can write a letter, report, etc. and send it to a lot of people at the same time, with each person's name and address in the letter.

9. **View:** In the View tab, you can switch between a single page and a double page. You can also change how the layout tools work. You can use it to make a print layout, outline, website, task pane, toolbar, and rulers, as well as to make a full-screen view, zoom in and out, and so on.

Creating a New Document

Create a New Document from the Blank Document or Preset Template

A document can be created either from the blank document or from the various available template that is available on MS word 365. After you are done creating the document, you can store such a document on your PC. To create the document from a blank document after you have launched into the program from the Microsoft website as we have discussed in the introduction, then:

A. Tap on the blank document, provided you have not been using the program before.
B. If you have been using the program before, click on the File menu.
C. Then tap on New.

Alternatively: after you have open the Word main screen, press Ctrl + N on the keyboard for new document shortcuts.

To start from the template, simply, click on any template of your choice from the available template, and it will be opened up.

Observing Microsoft Word Start Screen

Immediately, you launch to word 365, the first screen you will notice is known as the start screen, you can perform various activities with the start screen, as listed below:

1. The blank document is used to create a new document.

2. Featured is used to show various word online templates.

3. Personal is a link to show the templates you customize by yourself.

4. Type your desire template into the search box to run a check for you on the available template e.g (birthday format or Easter party).

5. Select a document from the group of the previous document you have accessed in a recent time.

6. Select a template from available offline templates.

7. Search for any other document inside your Word document.

Observing Microsoft Word Main Screen

The main screen shows the principal components of the word 365 Interface. Let us delve into those components:

1. **The title bar:** the title bar will show the name you use to save your document, the default name is document 1 if you have not used any name to save your document at all.
2. **Quick Access toolbar:** it contains a quick element that you can use to extract commands out of the available toolbar such as On/Off, save, undo, redo, etc.
3. **Tab:** a particular title or name given to each group of the ribbon.
4. **Ribbon:** it shows a group of connected commands under each tab.
5. **Command group:** this represents the gallery of related tools within tabs for instance within the Home tab, you will be having Editing, Fonts, Paragraph, and so on.
6. **Horizontal Ruler:** it is mainly used for measuring working areas horizontally.
7. **Vertical Ruler:** it is used for measuring the working area vertically.
8. **Cursor pointer:** it is where your typing entry will start from.
9. **Scroll bar:** it is used to scroll up and down within the document.
10. **Working area:** this is the largest area on the main screen, it is the area that will accommodate all your text entries.
11. **Status bar:** it gives an exact description of your documents, such as the number of pages and words.
12. **The view option:** the view option shows the current view option, such as Read mode, Print layout, and web layout.

13. **Zoom slider:** it is used to adjust (increasing or reducing) the size of the window screen.

Recognize Tabs and Ribbons

The essential aspect of the Word main screen is that of tabs and ribbons because that is where all MS word commands reside and use. Each word instrument is organized into Tabs and Ribbons, to perform any action, you will have to click on the Tabs where the group of related ribbons informs of the tool is kept, then click on each ribbon to initiate an action.

Note:

1. If you do not know the work of the ribbon, scan the ribbon by putting the cursor on top of the ribbon, and there will be a note of what the ribbon entails or do in its front.

2. The button or menu always has a downward pointing arrow indicating there are more tools inside, access them by clicking on the arrow.

3. The dialog box has various group functions, such as font, paragraph, style, etc. kindly, click on each right arrow to check the available group function in each dialog box group.

4. The file tab is known to be a backstage tab, when you click it, it will take you out of the main screen, when you are done with the file command, click the back arrow to return you to the main screen.

Ribbon Display Option (Hide and Unhide Ribbon)

The ribbon display option is used to adjust the option of a ribbon display to suit your preference, perhaps you want to create a lot of space for your working area, and thus, you may choose to hide the Ribbon or tab it depends. Ribbon display options are located at the top right corner of the Word window and it gives out 3 options when you click it, which are:

1. **Auto-hide Ribbon:** when you click on it, it hides both the tab and the ribbon.
2. **Show tabs:** it shows the tabs command and hides the ribbon command (but it is temporary as you click on it.
3. **Show tabs and commands:** it shows both tab and ribbon commands at once (some users preferred this as the best ribbon option).

Adjusting Ribbon Feature on Tablet Mode

The ribbon feature can be adjusted provided you have switched from desktop to tablet mode. The feature is simply the distance between the ribbons. Check below steps for ribbon space adjustment:

A. Tap on Customize Quick Access Toolbar button.

B. Select the Touch or Mouse mode to activate it.

C. Move to the right side of the (CQAT) and select either Mouse or touch mode.

Note: when you select the mouse option it will create little space between ribbons but the touch option will create more space between the ribbons.

Adjusting Document View Mode

MS Word gives you the privilege to adjust your document view mode to suit your preferences in the desktop window. It simply helps you view each part of your

document so you can adjust them as necessary. The normal mode is the print layout, which is the default way Word offers its document, placing a document on the screen with its four sides at the middle of the screen. It exposes the exact copy of what you will be having as a hard copy when you eventually print or broadcast the document. Let us examine the remaining view mode aside from print layout:

A. **Web layout:** this offers documents in the format of the web page, by occupying the whole window screen.

B. **Read mode:** Read mode presents the document in the format of the eBook, it hides almost all the tabs and ribbon except the file tabs.

C. **Draft:** this is the mode that allows seeing the plain text of the document, it hides certain formatting options such as header and footer and other objects.

D. **Outline:** as its name denotes, it outlines the document by arranging it by creating the actual heading and paragraph within the document.

There are two ways to switch between view modes, which are:

1. **Window screen switching:** you can switch between print layout, web layout, and read mode by touching any of the three modes located at the bottom right of the Word window.

2. **Using the View tab:** this grants you the opportunity to switch between any of the available modes including, draft and outline, simply tap on the View tab and click on any desire mode button.

Using Zoom Slider to Increase or Reduce the Appearance of the Text

Zoom sliders help to adjust the appearance of the text without unnecessarily increase the size of the text. Zoom magnification gives you the actual picture of how you want your text without adjusting the exact size of the text.

The fastest way of zooming the text is to make use of the Zoom slider at the lower right corner of the actual program window by adjusting the zoom magnification to the right to make text larger and to the left to make the text smaller.

To set the accurate zoom size:

A. Click on the percentage zoom button to open the zoom slider dialog box

B. Set the actual percentage by clicking on any of the percentage zoom text listed or you type it into the percentage text box if what you want is different from the one listed.

C. You can as well set the zoom text with page width, text width, and other criteria.

Note: For the desktop or laptop with the external mouse that has a wheel button, you can zoom the text by holding down the Ctrl button on the keyboard and keep rolling the mouse wheel up and down to zoom in and out respectively.

Formatting Text, Paragraphs, and Pages

Templates are already set pages that automatically create the kind of setting particular to whatever file type you're working with. Templates already have formats and layouts unique to them. For example, there are templates for agendas, brochures, business cards, envelopes, faxes, invitations, labels, invoices, etc.

In Word versions before this one, the several page layouts were set beneath the Page Layout panel. All you needed to do was to click one of them when you had to work with a different document type. However, now, with the new upgrade, it all changes. At the upper side of the Home Panel, you'd find a list of templates stacked in one row. A link also allows you to find more templates on the right side of the panel.

When you need to create a new project on word, you can click the blank file type if you don't have any template or page size requirement. That way, you can also make your specifications and alterations. However, if you want to create a project with specified size or dimension—for example, a business card, you might need to work with specific templates.

The template for a regular word document measures an inch away from the outermost edges, i.e., one inch from the left edge, one inch from the right edge, one inch from the upper edge, and one inch from the lower edge. You should also note that the default template for a regular word document is the portrait page orientation. The default font is Calibri; the default font size is 11pts, the default line spacing is multiple, and the line spacing is 1.08. You'd find a default line spacing of 1 inch for older Word versions.

Each template also has layout patterns and formatting tools peculiar to it. This means that when creating a brochure, for example, you don't have to worry about formatting your document so that it looks like a brochure. All you need to do is type and insert your pictures in between the text. Automatically, the software does the necessary editing and formatting.

If you check out the template list more closely, you'd also realize that some have borderlines, shades, watermarks, etc., fixed automatically to the documents. These features help you cut out a lot of stress while preparing your document. Here are some sources of these templates;

1. Templates already installed on your device. When you install Microsoft Word on your computer, you automatically access several templates.
2. You can get your templates from Office.com. However, these have to be downloaded first before they can be used. If you want to be sure the template is what you need, click the Preview tab.
3. You could also decide to be creative by creating your template! For this, you'd need to start from a normal Word document.

Let's see how you can open a Template and work with it.

1. Click the File icon on the upper panel.
2. Click New.

3. You get to see a long list of templates available on your computer. Click the Create icon, and click anyone you want to work with.

4. You immediately get directed to a new document configured to match the document's purpose.

You can conduct an online search if you do not find the template you want. Most times, you'd find some template prompts on your timeline. If none of those suit your document requirement, work with the Search Online Template Box. Type the keyword peculiar to the template and then click the Search icon. From there, you will find a longer list of templates that match the keyword entered.

Click any of the provided templates, and then, you'd get directed to a window that bears all the details about that template. From the preview window, you can also scroll through the list of templates by using the forward and back arrows. Once you decide on the template you want to work with, click Create.

You can also focus on how you can create a template that matches your project or file description. These techniques will be useful in a scenario where you do not find the very template you need. When you create a template, you will find it listed with the Customs Office Templates.

Let's get started with Custom Template Creation!

1. Open a new document using the regular standard—a blank document. If you want to do this on something you already created, you can go ahead.

2. Make your font settings, paragraph settings, page layout settings, and other document settings as required.

3. Pause with your changes and alteration processes. Save your document to your computer or the OneDrive cloud during that time. This way, you don't lose the changes made.

4. Click the Save As icon. You can change the document's name if you need to.
5. You will then be prompted to choose from a list of file types. The list is usually in the form of a drop-down menu. The file type for a template is (*.dotx).
6. Once you click that, the file you save will automatically join the Custom Template list.
7. Click the 'Save as' icon to finish the Template Creation process.

If you need to work with the saved template at a later date, all you need to do is;

- Click New.
- Afterward, click Personal.
- Choose the template type you want to work with.

The list you find depends on how many templates you created in the past. After clicking the template, you'd find a document based on those configurations. Now, even though templates seem pretty rigid in style and configuration, you can still get to make a couple of changes.

The newly fixed page has tools for page layout, page orientation, etc. The Home window also helps you have access to files and documents you recently worked with. You can easily work with the Search icon to scour through your recent files. The search spans your native file and those stored in the cloud. To open the document, all you need to do is right-click the recent file. You'd see a notification to that effect when you haven't worked on any file in a while.

You can also make a document the first thing you see by working with the Pin feature. All you need to actually do is highlight the file and click the Pin icon. The Share with Me list helps you have access to documents that you received from another party.

Adding Tables, Images, and Other Media

Creating and Working with Tables

Sometimes, when we are writing a document, we feel the need to organize our content better, and for this, we need to create a table. Word allows this to be done in the document very easily. With the tool, you can determine how many rows and columns you will have on it as well as if you want to merge any of the resources.

To insert a table, you will need to go to the insert tab and look for the second section, which says table. By clicking on the arrow that points down, you will select the squares that will determine how many fields you will have for each row or column. As you select, the top of the drop-down menu will show you the selected configuration. If you would rather select manually the number of columns and rows, you can click on insert table, and a dialogue window will open to allow you to place the number of columns and rows you want, the width of each column (that comes predetermined as fixed), and if you want it to fit automatically to the page. Here, you will also be able to determine if this is the standard you want for future tables.

Also, in this menu, you will have the opportunity to draw the table for yourself and add a really nice feature, that is to add an Excel spreadsheet to your document. Adding a spreadsheet to your document will make it easier to add calculations without risking making mistakes and using all the features of the program. It will also allow you to, as you will see next, to make graphs and charts to add to your document.

Pro tip: Once you insert a table, an extra tab will be added to the top menu named table tools. Here you will be able to determine the table design and the layout of your design, establish the style of the line, determine if you want to insert or delete a row, determine if there is a certain style you wish to add, sort the columns alphabetically, color a specific cell, and merge or split cells. Remember that all the other features you have already learned for the text are still applicable!

Graphs and Formulas

Suppose that the document you are creating is a business report that needs to present statistics and graphs. In that case, you can use Word to add these to your document. By going to the insert tab, you will find the option of adding illustrations—and one of them is a graph. Even if you do not have the data in an Excel spreadsheet, there is no need to worry. Once you select the button to add a chart, a dialogue box will open to choose the type you want to add. You can select from column charts to pie charts and even histograms in the preferences.

Once the type of chart you want has been selected, an image of the selected will appear together with an Excel spreadsheet. To make it actually even easier for you, the cells that will contain the information will already appear, naming everything that needs to be put into each box to generate the desired image. You will fill in the series and the labels according to your information. This spreadsheet, however, will not appear on your document. Once you are done filling in the information, your chart should update automatically, and you will need to press the x button to close it. Your changes will not be discarded.

Pro tip: To change the Excel spreadsheet information, click Edit Data. If the table you want to actually create already has the data in a different file, you can click on Select Data to choose where the information will come from. This will open a dialogue box to search your computer for the file.

As an added bonus, just like in the table feature, an additional tab will open every time you want to work with the chart: the Chart tools function. Clicking on it will enable the user to add chart elements, change the chart's layout, and even determine a style they want to be applied. You will also be able to choose the colors for the bars. If you want to make these changes manually and do not want to use any of the predetermined styles, you can do so in the Format tab of the chart tools.

To determine the size of your chart, you can either resize it by dragging one of the tips of the image (where there is a circle) up or down or enter the size on the height and width boxes on the ribbon. Now, suppose that you want this chart or graph to be aligned with the text, where the image will be on one side and the text on the other. Then, to do this, you will need to use the wrap text function. When you click on the downward-facing icon on the arrange tab, several options will be available with graphic images showing each of them where you want the image to be located.

Pictures, Shapes, and SmartArt

If you have already mastered the art of using graphs and charts and formatting them within your document, then images should not give you too much trouble. Although each of the categories mentioned in this section is a world of its own, you will see that there are relationships between each of them. All of these elements will come in handy when preparing a document that needs visual aids to help the reader better understand your point. To start off, let's talk about pictures.

Pictures

While you can use the keyboard shortcut to add a picture to the document you are writing (see shortcut keys at the end of this chapter), you can also insert one by using the ribbon. By going to the insert tab, you can add a picture from your computer or an online source. This will depend on your preference and if you have the image that you want stored on your device.

Once you have added the image, a new toolbar will appear on the ribbon that is specific to picture settings. If your chosen image needs corrections, you can use the corrections button in the adjust section. This part of the ribbon will allow you to edit the picture or perform any modifications you might need. There is also the possibility of resetting it in case there is something that you want to be undone.

Pro tip: If you do not want your image to be too heavy and make the document too big, you can click on the picture and then go to the compress image button. Here, you can determine if you want the compression to be done only to these pictures or all of those in the document (click or unclick on the box) and choose the resolution you want. Word will give you a small definition of each resolution so you can decide better which one you want to apply to it.

Another thing that you can do is manually adjust the picture. This can be done by moving and dragging it or determining the size you want in the box. In this section, you will also have the ability to crop the picture. Other features available are to rotate the image and determine its position and the position of the text next to it.

Pro tip: Many times, when we want to manually adjust the picture size, it becomes distorted since most of us have little control over how to maintain the width and the length of the image. To maintain the proportions of the original picture, all you need to do is keep the shift button pressed when you manually move it. This will allow the picture to maintain its original characteristics while still holding the proportion between length and width, avoiding distortion.

Shapes

To insert a shape into your document is similar to adding a picture. You will need to go to the ribbon and click on the shapes button in the insert tab.

Once you click the arrow pointing down, a section of all the available shapes will appear by category. Although the default is to have a shape that is painted inside and with colored borders, this can be easily changed in the shape format tab that will appear.

You can also move the shape's orientation by clicking on the round arrow that appears when you click on it. To choose the color of the line and the fill, if there is any that you want, you can go to these buttons on the ribbon and select them or select from one of the predetermined styles the software offers. Most of the same functions for regular picture work also for a shape, so it should be very straightforward.

You can also do it if you want to write inside the shape! All you need to actually do is click on it and start typing. Apply the text configuration available in the ribbon to format it the way you prefer. The position of the shape in reference to the text can also be determined by the text wrap box that will appear once you click on it.

Pro tip: Once you click on the arrow, several circles will appear on its borders. This is so you can format the shape to whatever format you would like. However, something to pay attention to is the yellow circles that appear. While the ones colored in white will allow you to resize the object, the ones in yellow will allow you to change their format. For example, if you are using the arrow shape, two yellow circles will appear—one at the beginning and one at the head of the arrow. If you move the one at the head of the arrow, you will be able to decide if you want it narrower or wider, while the rest of the arrow will remain the same. For resizing issues, use the same principle of pressing the shift button.

SmartArt

If there is one thing that Word can do to help the user, it's make the document easier to manipulate. With the SmartArt feature, you will be able to add processes, hierarchies, pyramids, and cycle images. To add one of these according to your necessity, do as you did with the two previous items and go to the insert tab on the ribbon. Select SmartArt, and a dialogue box will open with options for you to choose from. Here, you should choose the one that best fits your project and select it.

Once you have determined the best option for your file, it will appear by default colored and with the options of where to add the text.

Here the user can choose what to write, and the additional features are provided by a SmartArt tab that will appear on the ribbon. You will be able to add additional shapes, move the structure around, and change its colors. The text, as usual, will need to be defined in the Font toolbar.

Pro tip: Suppose you want to add a form to your created structure. In order for it not to be added to the end, select with your cursor which of the boxes (or forms) you want the additional element to be added to. If you just leave the structure clicked without selecting a specific shape, then it will be added to the end. However, if you select a specific element in the middle of the format and click on add shape, the shape will be automatically placed right after it, avoiding the rework of having to redo the whole format.

Collaborating on Documents in Real-Time

Collaborating on documents in real-time in Microsoft Word is a convenient and efficient way for multiple people to work on a document together, regardless of their physical location. Here are the basic steps for collaborating on a document in real-time in Microsoft Word:

1. **Share the document:** The first step is to share the document with the people you want to collaborate with. You can do this by emailing the document or by sharing it through OneDrive or SharePoint.

2. **Open the document:** Once the document has been shared, each collaborator can open it in Microsoft Word.

3. **Turn on real-time collaboration:** To turn on real-time collaboration, click on the "Share" button in the top right corner of the Word document. This will open a window where you can invite people to collaborate on the document.

4. **Invite collaborators:** To invite collaborators, enter their email addresses in the "Invite people" field and select the permission level you want to give them. You can choose between "Can edit" and "Can view" permissions.

5. **Work on the document:** Once the collaborators have been invited, they can work on the document in real-time. Each collaborator can see the changes made by others in real-time, and the document will update automatically.

6. **Review changes:** To review changes made by collaborators, click on the "Review" tab in the top menu bar of Word. This will allow you to view and accept or reject changes made by others.

7. **Save the document:** As collaborators work on the document, it is automatically saved in real-time. However, it is important to ensure that the document is saved periodically to avoid losing any changes.

In summary, collaborating on documents in real-time in Microsoft Word is a simple process that can be done by sharing the document with others and turning on real-time collaboration. With real-time collaboration, each collaborator can see changes made by others in real-time, allowing for a more efficient and effective collaboration experience. By reviewing changes and periodically saving the document, collaborators can ensure that their work is saved and preserved.

Excel

Introduction to Microsoft Excel

Microsoft Excel 2022 is a spreadsheet application and the most recent version of Excel software that helps users organise, manage, and add data using formulae. Furthermore, the software is part of the Microsoft Office suite, although it can also be used with other office programmes.

Like the bulk of other Microsoft programmes, Excel is available as a cloud-based subscription through Office 365. As an individual or a company, you can do more with Excel than you would realise. The software was created with Mac OS and Windows users in mind.

Both users can perform tasks such as constructing pivot tables, utilising graphing tools, and performing simple arithmetic. Excel also allows us to use the AVERAGE function and other functions to help us succeed at work. Workers who want to arrange and organise data can do so utilizing a collection of cells organized into columns and rows, which is available with Microsoft Excel 2022. Excel also displays data using histograms, charts, and line graphs.

What is Excel?

Excel is a Microsoft Office application that many people are familiar with. Because of its spreadsheet nature, it's widely applicable. Different kinds of data can be organized, calculated and kept data saved for future use. Excel grid interface allows you to organize virtually any type of data you can think of. Excel strength rests in its ability to let you design the layout and structure of the data you wish to organize, whatever you see fit. Microsoft Excel is the highly used spreadsheet in the world.

Excel spreadsheets allow you to work with tables of numerical data organized in columns and rows that can be modified using a wide variety of arithmetic operations and functions. With Excel, you can do simple calculations, use graphing tools, and build pivot tables, macro and many other useful things. They can also show data graphs, such as bar charts, histograms, and line graphs. Microsoft excel is compatible with different operating systems that include Mac, Android, Windows and IOS.

Organizing and manipulating data is easier using Microsoft Excel, which uses rows and columns. Numbers are used to representing spreadsheet rows, whereas alphabets are given to column headers. Excel may use Visual Basic for Applications (VBA) to program in Excel, and you can use DDE (Microsoft's Dynamic Data Exchange) to retrieve data from other sources.

Understanding The Purpose of Excel

Excel is a widely used Microsoft Office application commonly used by businesses and individuals to analyze and preserve numerical data. It is also a spreadsheet tool that allows consumers and businesses to record data and generate tables. Data analysis is straightforward with an MS Excel spreadsheet.

With graphs and charts, you may summarize data and keep it in an orderly manner so that you can easily retrieve it whenever you need it. It becomes simple to save data, and as a result, you will save a lot of time. MS Excel also allows users to utilize formulae to arrange, format, and calculate data in a spreadsheet system. MS Excel has a plethora of formulae.

You can use them to do multiple operations on a large amount of data simultaneously, such as computing the sum, average, and so on. As a result, MS Excel is employed whenever users need to solve complex mathematical problems or apply basic mathematical functions to large data sets. MS Excel includes many capabilities that can help you save time and make your job easier.

If you have data recorded in MS Excel and wish to highlight anything important, you can do it with the many data presentation choices available in MS Excel. You can even improve the appearance of the spreadsheets on which you've entered data. Budgeting can be done with MS Excel. If a freelancer earns $6,000 per month, for example, he will have certain expenses, and if he wants to actually know exactly how much he spends each month, he may simply do so with MS Excel.

He may record his monthly income and costs into excel tables, allowing him to see how much he is spending and, as a result, keep track of it. Excel is actually a part of the Microsoft Office suite and is interoperable with other Microsoft Office apps. Users can subscribe to Office 365 and purchase Microsoft Excel 2022 and prior versions on the cloud, just as other Microsoft Office products.

In addition, this software programme organizes and separates data using a cell collection structured into columns and rows. It can display data in charts, line graphs, and histograms. MS Excel has several advantages, which is why it is utilized by people worldwide for a range of activities. It not only saves time but also makes the job simpler. It's practically unstoppable in its ability to complete any assignment. You can, for example, make mathematical calculations and record data in graphs and charts. A businessperson can easily compute and save data in it.

Getting Started with Microsoft Excel

Microsoft Excel is a data analysis and representation programme that may be used to create a huge number of data sets, forecasts, and other accounting-related tasks. Accounting, financial, and calculating activities are only a few of the applications that can be applied. Excel has an appealing user interface and graphics and is frequently used.

Microsoft Excel 2022 also includes several new and innovative capabilities that make data entry, analysis, representation, and visualization simple and comprehensive. Excel may be used to tailor your data to whatever format you want using charts, shapes, icons, and numerous formatting tools.

Creating and Editing Spreadsheets

Once Excel has opened; your screen will look similar to the following:

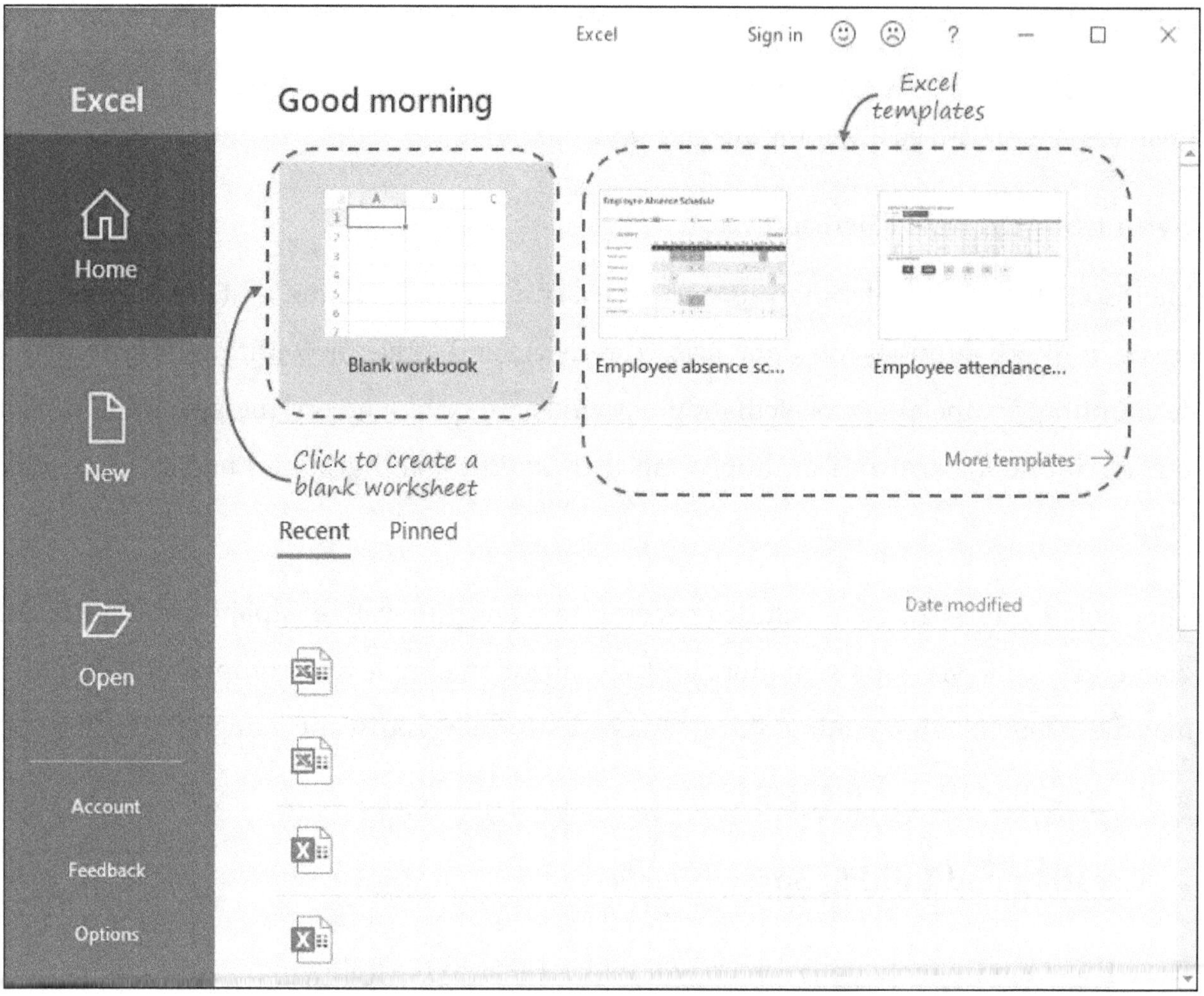

You'll notice pre-made templates available. The best practice is to first learn the basic functionality of Excel® before using these. Once you have a better understanding of Excel®, you may modify and verify the calculations in these templates meet your requirements.

Select the "Blank Workbook" option. After you click the option, you will have created a "workbook" file made up of one or more worksheets. The entire screen is displayed for easier viewing:

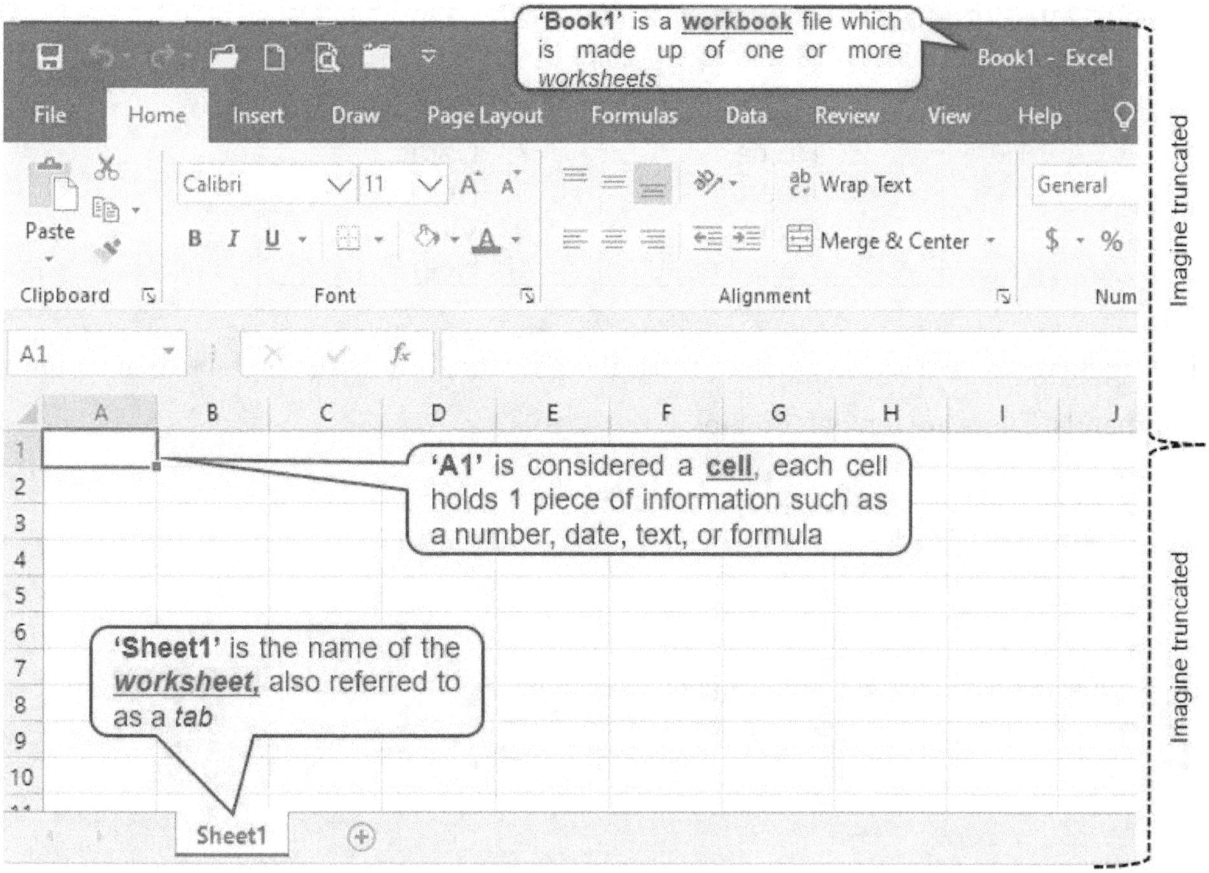

- **Workbook**

A workbook file is made up of one or more worksheets. Worksheets are also referred to as tabs.

- **Worksheet**

A worksheet is made of up cells displayed in a grid of rows and columns.

- **Cell**

A cell holds one piece of information such as a number, currency value, date, text, or formula.

Next, let's review how to navigate and customize the toolbar (Ribbon) and quick access toolbar.

- **Toolbar (Ribbon)**

1. File	6. Formulas
2. Home	7. Data
3. Insert	8. Review
4. Draw	9. View
5. Page Layout	10. Help

The toolbar, or what Microsoft® calls the "ribbon," consists of tabs that contain commands. There are ten default tabs.

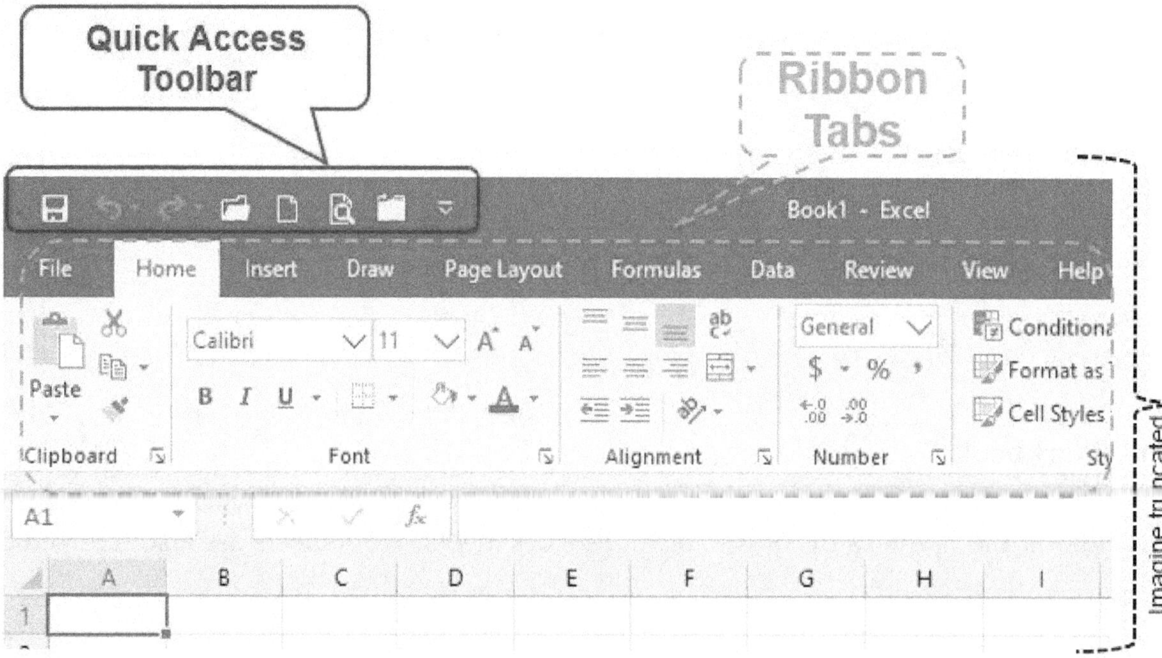

Working with Formulas and Functions

What You Should Know About Excel Formulas

Excel relies heavily on formulas. You should learn how to write formulas in your spreadsheet that perform calculations, combine values, and refer to specific cells.

Types of Formulas

Arithmetic, financial, and look-up formulas are the three types of calculation formulas available in Excel. A specific function key is assigned to each of these formulas.

Arithmetic Formulas

Arithmetic formulas are used to perform calculations and determine numerical operations' outcomes. Simple math functions and common arithmetic operators (such as +, -, *, /) are the most commonly used arithmetic formulas in Excel. These functions are also available in the calculator of your word processor.

Financial Formulas

Financial Formulas Financial formulas use money values such as interest rates and percentages to calculate financial transactions. You'll need to know how to use some financial formulas in formulas that work with these values before learning how to write financial formulas in Excel.

Look-Up Formulas

Look-up formulas are used to find information such as a company's financial statement size or year, or the cost of gasoline in five different states. INDEX, MATCH, and IFERROR are the most commonly used look-up formulas in Excel. These functions determine the results of locating data in a range or table.

How to Work with Formulas

A formula can be typed or copied from another cell and pasted into a cell. These instructions will show you how to enter data into a cell and how to enter formulas.

Type information into a cell.

Click in a cell and type = to enter a formula (equal sign).

Type the formula's components (arguments), such as values and operators, in the formula bar.

To finish, press "Enter."

Go to the cell and click "Formula" to see the result of your formula. The Formula bar shows the result of your formula.

You should be aware of the following things before learning how to write formulas:

Defining Functions in Excel

A function is a collection of instructions that perform a calculation or action on the contents of a cell. An argument is a formula that is enclosed in parentheses. Any number of arguments can be passed to a function, but the function determines the number and types of arguments.

User-defined (formulas) and built-in functions are the two types of functions available in Excel (built-in functions).

User-Defined Functions

A user-defined function is a piece of code that you write yourself. Visual Basic for Applications (VBA), the programming language for Excel and other Office applications, is used to create the code. Then you run the VBA macro to see the worksheet's results of your function.

Built-in Features

Excel's built-in functions are formulas that perform various tasks on cells. The majority of them are simple mathematical formulas, but some can do more complicated things like look up data in a table.

The following are the characteristics of built-in functions:

- They are suitable for use in any worksheet.
- They are simple to use and comprehend.
- They can be moved from one workbook to the next.

- They have "built-in" error checking, which means that if you make a mistake in your function, Excel will display an alert dialogue box and stop executing it.
- Excel does not allow you to create new built-in functions. You can either use the ones already there or later add them to a custom toolbar.
- The first letters of the function are used to name them.
- In most Excel versions, they perform the same functions.
- They may have functions that return values and use a set of arguments that you specify.
- You can use one or more arguments depending on the type of function.

Learning About Arguments

The values you put inside the parentheses in a formula are the arguments for a function. The function calculates its results using the arguments. When you create a function, you must specify all required arguments, but you can usually leave any optional arguments empty.

Example of arguments:

=Sum(A1:B10) =Sum(A1:B10) =Sum(A1:B10) =Sum(A1:B10) = (Number1, ...)

The arguments in the formula above are as follows:

Number1 - This argument is the input range, which can be an array formula. If you want to sum cells A1 through A10, type =sum (A1:A10). These arguments represent the other input ranges for your formula.

The result will be a single cell with the sum of each range's values (column C's sum) (sum of B column).

=Date(year,month,date)

The first argument in the formula is the date to be found, while the second argument is the year, month, and date.

FV= (rate, nper, pmt, pv, [fnce])

The following arguments are specified in the formula above: rate — the interest rate for this payment is determined by this argument. nper — specifies the number of payments to be made. pmt — the amount of each payment is set with this argument. pv —the current unpaid balance is set by this argument. [fnce] - if an optional argument is not specified, brackets ([]) must be used to indicate that it is optional.

=if(logical test,value if true,[value if false])

The following arguments are used in the formula above:

x: The logical test's outcome can be either "true" or "false."

value if x: When the variable x is true, the formula returns this value. If it returns false, the argument will be removed from the formula.

#N/A: This indicates that this argument does not have a value.

Formulas in Excel: Why Do You Need Them?

You'll use formulas in Excel for a variety of reasons.

- The first is that it actually allows you to see the results of a calculation or action directly on your worksheet. This can assist you in making more informed decisions and maintaining control over the actions in your worksheet.
- The second reason is that you may want to use variables in your calculations, such as the number of sales or daily sales, to change these numbers without having to change all of your formulas.
- The third reason is that performing calculations in a workbook can assist you in managing multiple worksheets. For example, you might need to enter data for your vendors, customers, and employees in a business bookkeeping application. If you do this in one worksheet, you'll have to double-check and update the data

in all the others. After entering data into the first worksheet, you can easily update those values using functions, and all other customer, sales, and employee records will be updated automatically.

- The fourth reason is if you want to create your functions by combining different parts of Excel and using a variety of Excel features. For example, you can create a custom date field in your worksheet using an Excel formula to perform a calculation on the New Year's date.
- The fifth reason is that, even if you don't use formulas in Excel, the workbook displays formulas and comments every time you save it, which is useful for programmers and document maintainers.

Key Information to Know About Functions

There are five key points I'd like to share with you:

- Because functions can be quite long, be careful what you type into the cell. The function's argument, or argument, is the function enclosed in parentheses. For example, the formula =COUNT(A:B:D) refers to the range A:B:D.
- Text can also be included in functions (words). When you actually copy a formula from one cell to another, Excel pastes the text instead of replacing it with numbers in the formula.
- Excel displays a #NAME? error in the cell if you create a formula with incorrect spelling or syntax. Only when you correct the error does the formula work.
- Because it can represent any value, the question mark (?) is known as a wildcard. When Excel replaces the question mark with a value, it performs the calculations you specified in your function formula on that value.

Excel displays the results of your function and its arguments when you press F4 on a cell with a formula. "Displaying the formula" is the term for this. You can also press F4 in the formula bar to see information about your function.

What You Should Know About Excel Functions

What does Function Mean in Excel?

EXCEL FUNCTION is a formula that has certain values in a certain order. One of the features is used for quick operations such as adding up a number and finding the sum. It can also be used to figure out how many cells are in a group and how many are the highest or the lowest. In cell A3, for example, the SUM function is used to figure out the sum of a range from A1 to A2.

Adding up all of the numbers in a list is what SUM does.

A phrase called AVERAGE is used to figure out the average number from a group of numbers.

To count the number of things in a set, use COUNT.

Why Functions Are Important in Excel

Excel functions make it easier for people to work with the programme.

Assume that you want to determine how much the above-mentioned home supply budget costs. A method can help you figure out the number. To call cells E4 through E8 one at a time, you'd have to use a formula. = E4 + E5 + E6 + E7 + E8 + E9 + E10 + E11 + E12 is the sum of these things.

If you use a function, the above formula will be written as =Sum if you write it down (E4:E8)

To get the sum of a group of cells, you can use a function rather than a formula, which would have to look at a lot of different cells. You can actually see how this works in the above function.

When you think about it, the function is really a formula that does different value calculations in a certain order. If you want to quickly figure out the sum, count, average, lowest value, and highest value of a group of cells, Excel has many different functions that can be used to do that quickly. To work with functions correctly, you'll need to know about all of the parts of a function and how to make arguments for measuring values and cell references so that you can work with them the right way.

The Parts of a Function

In order for a feature to work effectively, it must be written in a specific style, which is known as syntax. The typical syntax for a function is the equals sign (=), the function name (for example, SUM), and one or more arguments. Arguments include the information you want to measure. The function will sum the values from cells A1 to A20 in the example below.

Using arguments in your work

Parentheses must surround arguments and apply to all actual cells and cell ranges. You can provide one or more arguments depending on the syntax required for the feature.

For example, the feature =AVERAGE(B2:B9) calculates the average of the numbers in the B1:B9 cell set. This function only takes one argument.

To distinguish between numerous arguments, a comma must be used. For example, the function =SUM(A2:A3,C1:C3,E1) adds the values of three arguments' cells.

How to Create Functions?

You can use a variety of functions in Excel. Here are a few useful functions that are frequently used:

SUM: This feature adds up all of the values in the cells of the argument.

AVERAGE: The average of all the values in the statement is calculated using this equation. It adds the sums of the cells in the statement and divides the result by the number of cells in the statement.

COUNT: This feature counts the number of numerically detailed cells in the statement. This function can be used to actually count the number of items in a cell range quickly.

MAX: This feature returns the value of the largest cell in the argument.

MIN: This feature returns the value of the lowest cell in the argument. To use the AutoSum command to establish a function, follow these steps:

The AutoSum command inserts the most popular functions, such as Amount, AVERAGE, COUNT, MIN, and MAX, into your formula automatically. We'll use the SUM feature to measure the net expense of a collection of recently purchased products in the illustration below.

1. Choose the cell where the function would be stored. We'll go with cell D13 in this scenario.

2. Press the arrow key next to the AutoSum function on the Home page's Editing group. Then choose the required feature from the drop-down menu. We'll go with Sum in this scenario.

3. Excel may automatically insert the feature into the column and select a cell set for the statement. In our situation, the contents of cells D3–D12 were automatically picked, and their contents will be summed to calculate the overall expense. If Excel selects the erroneous cell range, you must manually enter the relevant cells into the statement.

4. Press the Enter key on your keyboard. The function will run, and the result will be displayed in the cell. In our situation, the number of D3:D12 is $765.29.

The AutoSum command can also be found in the Formulas area of the Ribbon

You should use the Alt+= keyboard shortcut instead of the AutoSum command. Hold down the actual Alt key and click the equals symbol to use this shortcut.

How do I manually enter a function?

You can just type it in if you already know the feature name. In the image below, we'll utilise the AVERAGE function to get the average amount of things sold by each battalion (a count of cookie sales).

1. Select the cell where you actually want the function to be saved. Cell C10 will be our choice in this situation.

2. Type the equals symbol (=) followed by the name of the function you want to utilise. You can also select a function from a list of suggested functions that shows below the cell when you type. In our example, we'll type =AVERAGE. Type the cell range for statement inside parentheses. We'll sort in this scenario (C3:C9). The values from cells C3 to C9 are added together, then divided by the total number of contents in the range.

3. Press the Enter key on your keyboard. The function will run, and the result will be displayed in the cell. In this case, the average number of units sold from each soldier is 849.

Because Excel doesn't always tell you if your calculations are correct, it's up to you to double-check them.

The Function Library

Even though Excel has hundreds of functions, the ones you'll need the most will depend on the type of data in your workbooks. There's no need to master every function; nonetheless, understanding some of the many types of functions can help you establish new ventures. You can also use the Feature Library on the Formulas list to search for functions by category, such as Financial, Text, Logical, and Date & Time.

1. To access the Function Library, go to the Ribbon and select Formulas. Look for the Function Library group.
2. Follow these steps to use a functionality from the Function Library:
3. In the illustration below, we'll utilise the COUNTA feature to count the total number of objects in the Items column. COUNTA, unlike COUNT, will tally cells that contain data other than numerical data.
4. Decide which cell will be used to store the function. We'll pick cell B17 in this situation.
5. Select the Formulas tab on the Ribbon to access the Function Library.
6. From the Function Library group, select the required feature type. We'll select Further Functions and then hover over Statistical in this example. Select the appropriate element from the drop-down menu. In this example, we'll utilise the COUNTA feature to count the particular number of cells in the Items column that aren't empty.

The Function Arguments dialogue box will display. From the drop-down option, choose Value1, then type or click in the appropriate cells. In our example, we'll get to cell range A3:A12. You can keep adding arguments to the Value2 region, but in this case we only want to actually count the number of cells in the A3:A12 range.

When you're finished, click OK.

The procedure will occur, and the result will be displayed in the cell. In our example, the outcome demonstrates that a total of ten things are arranged.

Formatting Cells and Worksheets

One of the main things you actually need to know when using Excel is how to format the cells so that they work for you. You have already seen how to change the format and color of the cells, so we will jump right into the program's specifics.

Number and Style

When you go to the home tab, you will see a section titled number. There will be a drop down menu for quick formatting, or you can click on the arrow on the right corner of the section to open the dialogue box. To start off, we recommend doing it this way so that you can visualize the options. Remember that to format the cell, it needs to be selected. Depending on your need, you can format one or more cells at once.

Once the dialogue box is open, you will be able to decide what kind of format you want the content of the cell to be shown in. This is important because it will directly affect the calculations that you perform. You can choose between several styles, including a time format, and a custom one. Here, the suggestion is to explore each one of them to get more acquainted with the program. Other types of formatting that can be done in this menu include alignment, font, border, fill, and the protection of the cell.

Pro tip: If you plan on sharing your spreadsheet and do not want people to modify a specific cell or group of cells, you can use the option to lock the cell. Once you click on this option in the Protection tab of the dialogue box, the program will automatically identify that this cell needs to be protected. To finalize the process, you should go to the review tab and click on the protect sheet option. A new dialogue box will open where you can select what you want to protect, and it will request a password that will be needed in case the user wants to modify the locked data.

Conditioning Formatting

This is one of the best functions to use once you start doing calculations. It will allow Excel to format the cells with a specific value automatically. Using it is very easy—click on the conditional formatting button on the home tab and select a new rule. A dialogue box will open where you can choose what you want to format, such as the option to format cells containing certain aspects. Suppose you click on this option: The bottom part of the dialogue box will change, and you will be able to set the rule for your worksheet or selected cells, rows, or columns. Once you have set the rules based on the assistant, you can click on the format button and decide what these cells look like. Remember to select the cells you want to apply this to before doing so.

In case you want to delete certain rules or view what are the ones being used in the spreadsheet, you can go back to the same conditional formatting button and click on the relevant options. Other ways of applying conditional formatting on your worksheet is to apply color scales, icons, data bars, and ranking. All of these are found in the drop-down menu of the function and have assistants to aid you in what style you want to apply.

Other Formatting Tips

Once you get a handle on how to manage the cells, everything else will become easier. Here are a few formatting tips that might be useful:

- **Use the paintbrush:** Use the paintbrush tool to format all of your cells according to the style you want. If you need more tips on how to use it, refer to Chapter 1 under the formatting section.

- **Series or repetition:** If you want to copy the same content to the next line or row, you do not need to write them manually or copy and paste. Go with the mouse on the bottom-right corner of the cell with the original text, and you will see that a cross symbol appears. Click on it with the mouse and drag until the place where you want the series or the repetition to continue, and the system will automatically do it. Once you are done, a small box will open next to it, and you can choose from the options what you want to do with it, including filling in the series or only repeating the formatting.

- **Moving a cell:** You can also choose to relocate a cell from its original location. In this case, rather than bringing your mouse to the bottom right-hand corner, you first select the cell and then click on any of its lines. A cross with four arrows will appear. You should then click on it with the mouse and drag it to where you wish to take it to. The formatting will go along with it.

Pro tip: When moving or replicating the cells, beware that if they are formatted or contain formulas, these will remain. However, if your cell is a part of a formula, this might change the results, and you might need to go to the cell where the calculation is being done and change the information on the row and the column where the information is.

- **Date formatting:** Out of all the formatting tips, the most confusing is regarding dates. If your cell is not set to the general or the date style, a number will appear when you type in the information. This is because the software recognizes the date but will return to you which day number it is since January 1, 1900. Therefore, do not worry if your cell is set to number formatting and you type it in, and a number appears—all you need to do is format the cell, which will appear in the correct format. The standard for the software will be day/month/year. To change this, go to the dialogue box under the number and change it according to the order you wish.

- **Line break:** Excel allows you to do this if you are typing in a text, and you do not actually want it to be a full line but rather a broken text. On top of the worksheet, you will see a line that says fx where the text of that cell is placed (or where you will type in the formulas). Type in the text in this field, and to decide where you want to break the text into more than one line, use Alt+Enter. This will automatically bring the cursor to the next line. You may do this as you wish.

Pro tip: To have the cell automatically adjust to the content, you can also use the Wrap text function located in the Alignment section of the home tab. This will automatically adjust the content to the current column width of the spreadsheet while increasing the space on the lines. The cells will automatically format themselves if you use the tip on the line break section.

Creating Charts and Graphs

[Text here]

Excel Charts

A chart is a graphical or visual representation of data in a worksheet in such a way that the users can have a better understanding of the data rather than just looking at the numbers. Excel provides different kinds of chart formats that match what you want.

Types of Charts

- **Column Charts**

Column charts are useful for data in both row and column forms. Column charts are ideal when you wish to show changes to data over time or wish to compare specific subsets of data. The average column chart places categories on the X-axis and values on the Y-axis.

- **Bar Charts**

Bar charts are quite similar to column charts and share all the same subtypes. Bar charts are useful when it comes to illustrating how individual items compare to one another. When it actually comes to choosing between the two, consider a bar chart when working with durations of time as your values or when the axis labels are longer than average.

- **Line Charts**

Line charts are a useful method of displaying data continuously over a specific amount of time. Typically, it is used to show how multiple variables performed along a set scale when compared to one another. Any data that is placed into rows or columns can be turned into a line chart and the X-axis holds category data and Y-axis contains the value data. Line charts are especially useful when various category labels are written as text and are spread out evenly such as quarters, months, or years.

- **Scatter Chart**

Scatter charts are also able to change the scale of the horizontal axis to deliver a greater degree of specificity. It is also useful when you actually want to use a horizontal axis with a logarithmic scale, when the X values are easily segmented or when there are more than 10 points on the X-axis. It is also a great choice when you want to display numerous data points where time is not a factor. To prepare data for being put into a scatter chart, it is important to place all of the values that you want to be graphed on the X-axis in a single column or row and then enter the Y-axis values in the next column or row.

- **Pie Chart**

For data that can be expressed in a single column or row, the best choice to display it visually is typically a pie chart. Pie charts are typically used to show individual parts of a whole in relation to the combined total of all of the parts in question. The percentage of each category's contribution will also be displayed as a percentage. Pie charts are the perfect choice when none of the relative values are negative, none of the values are zero, there are no more than seven categories being graphed and, most importantly, all of the values are related to a larger whole.

- **Area Charts**

Area charts are useful for making the magnitude of a category's values change over time more readily visible. They are also an easy way to emphasize each value in relation to the whole. Area charts typically show a variety of plotted values as well as their sum total.

Customizing Charts

After creating a chart, you have several tools available for formatting and customizing the chart to your liking. For example, you can swap the axis, change/adjust the data source, update the chart title, adjust the layout, apply a chart style, and apply a theme color to your chart.

To demonstrate some of these options, let's say we need to create a chart with four quarters of sales.

	A	B	C	D	E
1	Sales by Quarter				
2	Product	QTR1	QTR2	QTR3	QTR4
3	Chai	300	300	200	400
4	Beer	300	200	400	300
5	Coffee	350	400	500	500
6	Green Tea	250	150	100	300
7	Tea	100	400	100	500
8	Chocolate Biscu	320	200	100	300
9	Scones	250	500	200	100
10	Brownie Mix	350	400	550	200
11	Cake Mix	200	370	300	200
12	Granola	250	100	200	400
13	Hot Cereal	350	500	300	200
14	Chocolate	350	200	300	300
15	Fruit Cocktail	200	230	250	200
16	Pears	100	200	300	450
17	Peaches	200	300	200	600
18					

To create the chart:

Select the range with the data, including the column headers and row headers.

Click on Insert > Recommended Charts. You're presented with the Insert Chart dialog box with several chart recommendations for your data.

Select the Clustered Column option.

Click OK.

A chart will be created and added to your worksheet.

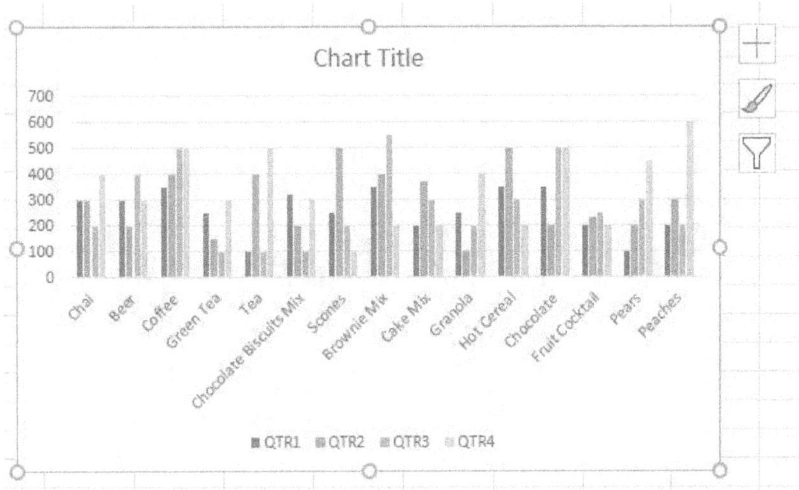

- **Switching the X and Y Axes**

You can switch the values Excel applies to the vertical axis (also called the Y-axis) and horizontal axis (also called the X-axis).

To switch the values applied to the axes:

Select the chart.

Click Chart Design > Switch Row/Column.

This will swap the values applied to the vertical and horizontal axes.

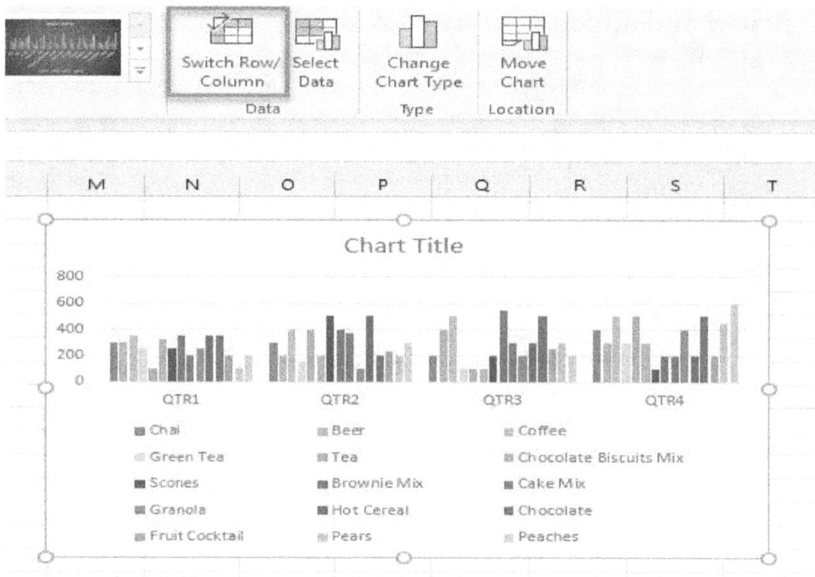

To swap the values back, simply click the Switch Row/Column button again.

- **Change the Data Source**

To change the data used as the source of the chart, do the following:

Click the Select Data button on the Design tab. The Select Data Source dialog box will actually be displayed.

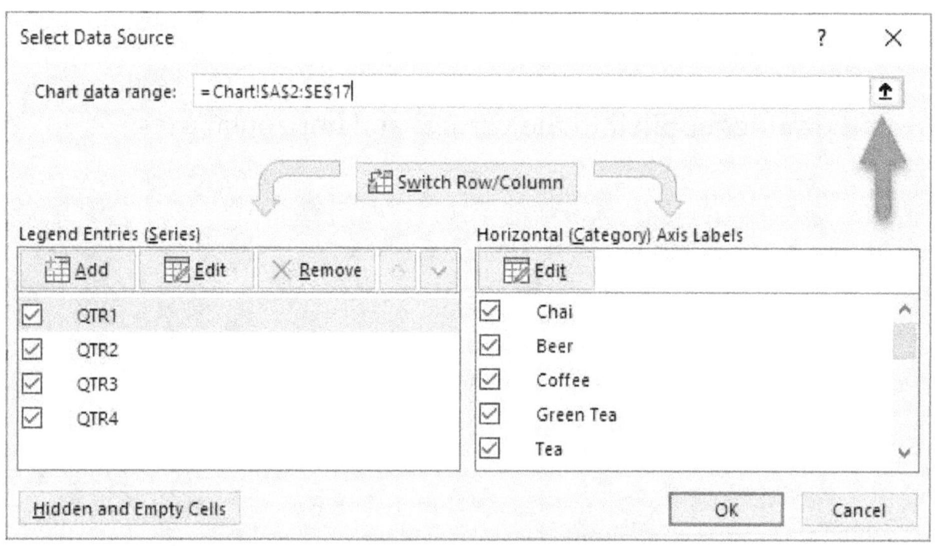

Select the up arrow that is on the Chart data range field. This will change it to a down-pointing arrow.

Select the cells you want in the worksheet area and click on the down-pointing arrow to return to the Select Data Source screen.

Click OK to confirm the change.

The new data source will now be used for the chart.

- **Adding Axis Titles**

When you create a new chart, you'll see "Chart Title" as a placeholder that needs to be edited with the title of the chart. There are also no labels at the axis, and we may want to add them to the chart.

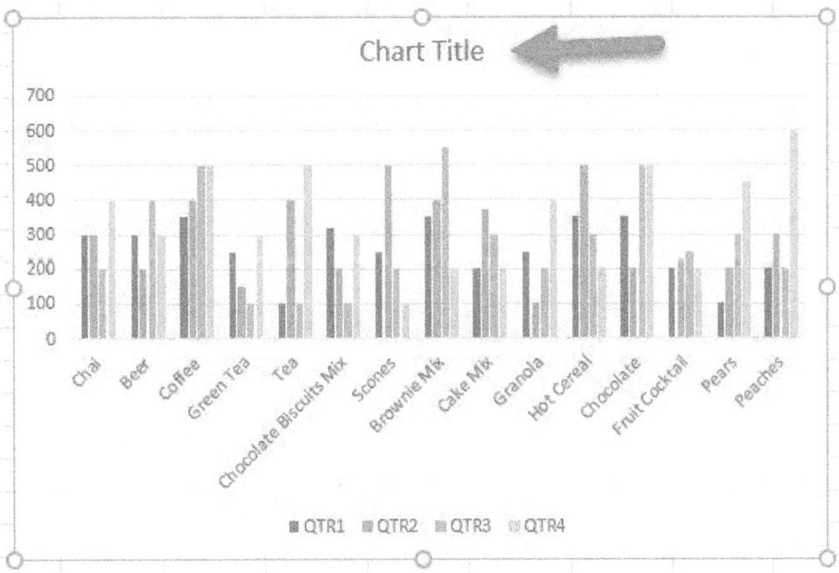

To change the Chart Title, you can simply click on it and type in the title. Alternatively, you can select the name from a field on your worksheet. For example, if we wanted our chart title to be Sales by quarter, which is in cell A1 of our worksheet, we would click on the Chart Title label and in the formula bar, enter "=A1". This will use the value in cell A1 for our chart title.

We can also add titles down the left-hand side and at the bottom of the chart. These are called axis titles. The left side is the Y-axis while the bottom is the X-axis.

To change the layout of your chart, click on Chart Design > Quick Layout.

You'll get a pop-up with several chart layouts. With the chart selected, you can mouse over each layout to view more details about it and get a preview of how your chart will look with that layout. A few of the options provide axis titles as well as move the legend to the right of the chart. If you want a layout with both axis titles, then Layout 9 would be a good pick.

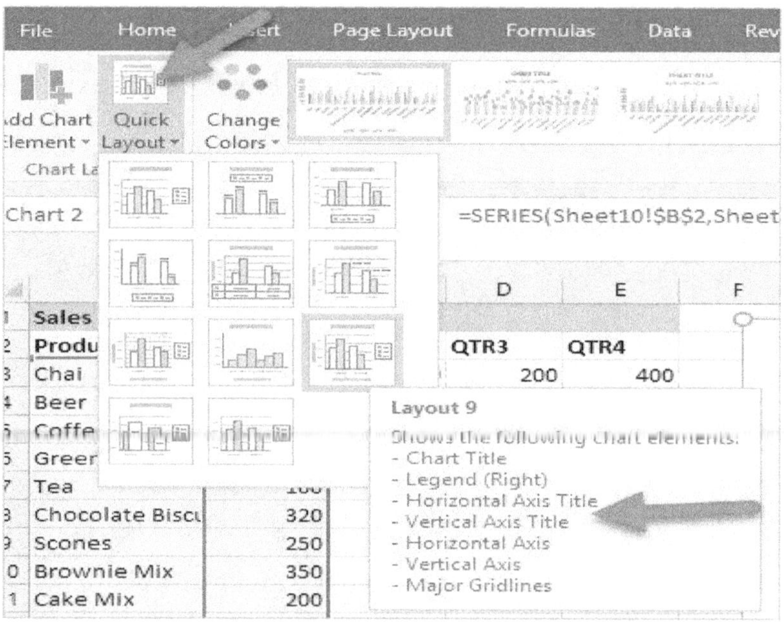

If we select Layout 9, we get a chart with labels that we can edit to add titles to the X-axis and Y-axis.

You can edit the axis labels as described above. You can click on the labels and type in the text directly or pull the text from your worksheet area by typing in a cell reference, for example, =A1, assuming cell A1 as the text you want for that label.

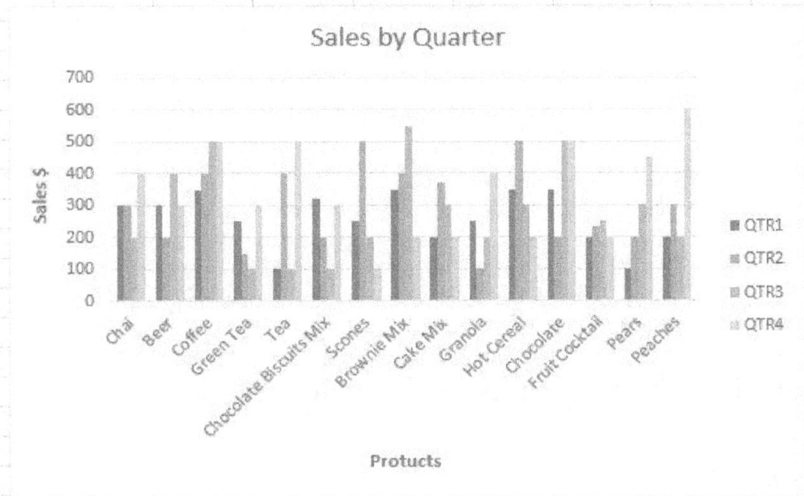

- **Chart Styles**

When you click on the chart, the Chart Design tab shows up on the Ribbon. On this tab, you have an array of Chart Styles you can choose from to change the look and color of your chart.

To change the color of the actual plot area:

Click on the plot area to select it (this is the center of the chart) and it will be selected.

With the plot area selected, click on the Format tab on the Ribbon.

Click the drop-down button in the Shape Styles group.

You'll get a pop-up with many Theme Styles to choose from for the format of the plot area. You can mouse over each one to see a preview of how your chart would look like if selected.

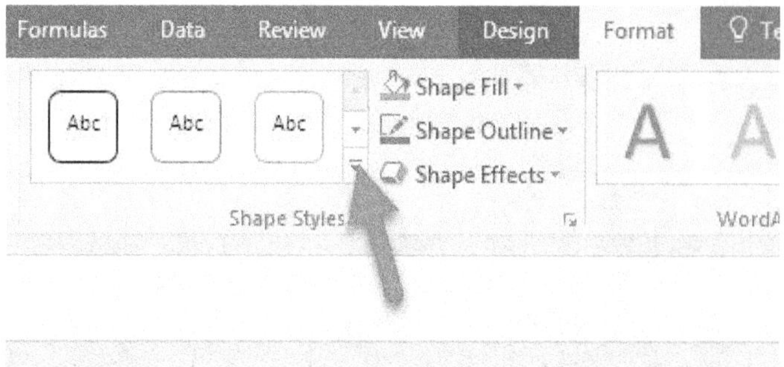

When you actually find the one you like, click on it to select it.

Creating Sparkline Charts

- **Adding a Sparkline**

Select the data you want to create a Sparkline chart for. At the lower-right corner of the selection, you'll see the Quick Analysis tool.

Click on the Quick Analysis tool to open a pop-up menu of Quick Analysis options—Formatting, Charts, Totals, Tables, and Sparklines.

Click on Sparklines and then select one option from Line, Column, or Win/Loss.

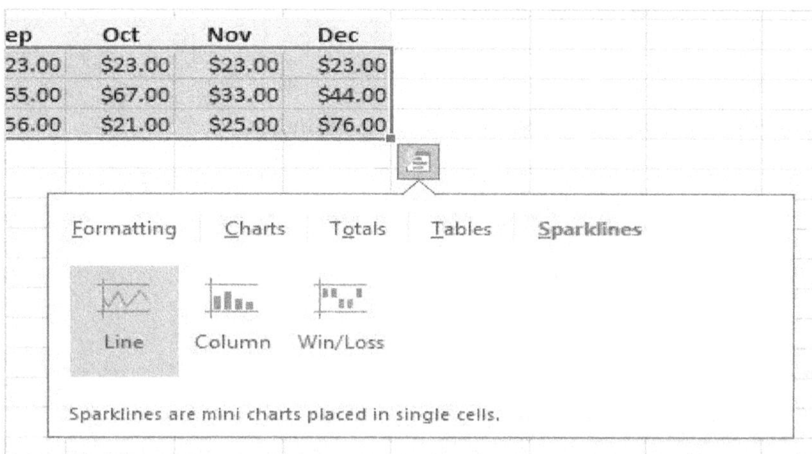

For this example, the Line option was selected. The sparklines will be created in the cells immediately to the right of the selected values.

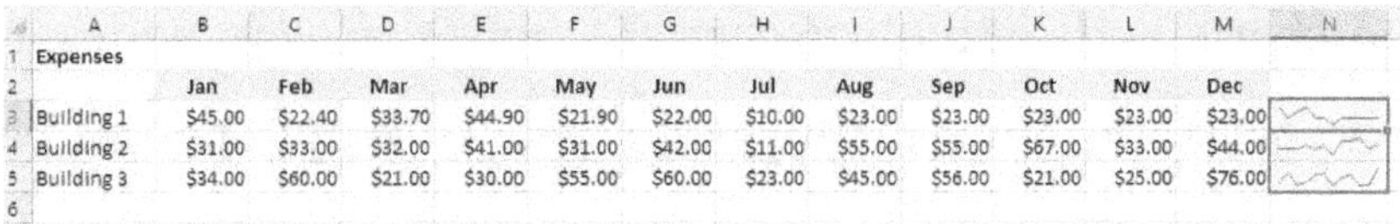

	A	B	C	D	E	F	G	H	I	J	K	L	M	N
1	Expenses													
2		Jan	Feb	Mar	Apr	May	Jun	Jul	Aug	Sep	Oct	Nov	Dec	
3	Building 1	$45.00	$22.40	$33.70	$44.90	$21.90	$22.00	$10.00	$23.00	$23.00	$23.00	$23.00	$23.00	
4	Building 2	$31.00	$33.00	$32.00	$41.00	$31.00	$42.00	$11.00	$55.00	$55.00	$67.00	$33.00	$44.00	
5	Building 3	$34.00	$60.00	$21.00	$30.00	$55.00	$60.00	$23.00	$45.00	$56.00	$21.00	$25.00	$76.00	
6														

To format your Sparkline chart, click on it to select it.

On the Ribbon, click on the Sparkline tab. In the Style group, you'll see various options to edit and style your sparkline chart.

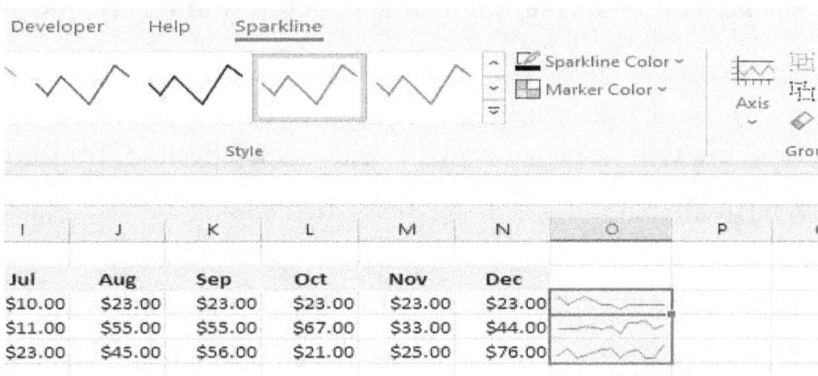

Use the following options to design your sparkline:

On the Sparkline tab, click on Line, Column, or Win/Loss buttons to change the chart type.

You can check Markers to highlight specific values in the Sparkline chart.

You can actually select a different Style for the Sparkline.

You can change the Sparkline Color and the Marker Color.

Click on Sparkline Color > Weight to change the width of the Sparkline.

Click on Marker Color to change the color of the markers.

Click on Axis to show the axis, if the data has positive and negative values.

Add/Remove Chart Titles

Adding titles to charts and individual charts X and Y axes provides an easy way to make complex information more readily apparent. Title options can be found under Chart Tools once a chart has been selected to allow access to the Format, Layout, and Design tabs.

To actually add a title to a chart, select the Layout tab and the grouping of options titled Labels to find the Chart Title option.

A box will appear labeled Box Title, fill it in and determine where you want the title to be placed.

Text formation options will appear once the text is highlighted; traditional formatting options will also be available.

To add titles to the axes, start by selecting the preferred chart and then viewing the Layout tab, the Labels grouping of options, and the option labeled Axis titles.

This option will provide you with the opportunity to label all the axes including multiple X or Y axes. To add a title for the Z-axis, select the option labeled Depth Axis Title.

Enter a title and you will be provided with formatting options as well.

Adding Data Point Labels

Individual labels can be added to specific data points in some charts to emphasize specific areas of importance.

To add a single label to all data points in a specific series or a single point in a series, start by selecting the desired chart to pull up the Chart Tools option.

Select the layout tab, followed by the Labels grouping of options and the option for Data labels.

This will actually provide you with options when it comes to naming an individual or multiple labels as well as removing unneeded labels.

Add a Legend

A legend is a quick and easy way to ensure that everyone viewing your chart knows exactly what they are looking at.

To add a legend to a specific chart, start by selecting the desired chart to pull up the Chart Tools option.

Select the Layout tab and the grouping of options titled Labels to find the Legend option.

Select the options related to your specific graph, additional options are available under the More Legend Options button.

Legend adjustments can be made through this window or by dragging the legend using the mouse. Adjustments made through the options menu will automatically populate and make adjustments to data placing as needed.

Selecting the legend and hitting the delete key will remove the legend from the chart.

Selecting the individual legend entries will allow you to edit them individually.

Modify Chart Size

Charts can be moved or resized by simply dragging them as required.

Charts can also be resized from the Format tab by selecting the Size grouping of options, then Shape Width, and Shape Height.

Additional options are located in the same place on the ribbon under the button next to the Size label. Here you will be able to actually determine if you want the chart to scale, rotate, or be resized.

The properties tab provides controls regarding how the chart moves in relation to how cells are resized in the worksheet.

Create a Chart Template

Start by selecting the chart that you will want to save for future use.

Select the Design tab and look for the grouping of options labeled Type and choose the Save as Template option.

By default, after you enter a name for the template, it will be viewable under the Templates option in the Insert Chart menu.

Giving the template a name and saving it will populate future charts with all of the colors, format, and height and width specifications as the original. It can then be modified as normal.

The template will be available across worksheets and workbooks.

Analyze Data in Excel

In every field, Microsoft Excel is among the most widely used techniques. Others stick to basic pie charts and conditional formatting, while others love experimenting with pivotal tables and histograms.

Some can transform the dull monochrome Excel into a piece of art, whereas others may be content with its data processing. In this discussion, we'll take a close look at Microsoft Excel and its capabilities. We'll go into how to process data in Excel Analytics and some tips and tricks. The topic would also look at how to interpret data in Excel in different forms.

Make Pivot Table

We may use a pivot tool to summarize large volumes of data. It is often used to explain and identify trends in data collection and is one of the most straightforward approaches to analyze data in Excel.

Pattern recognition in a minimal sample is straightforward. However, due to the size of the databases, finding similarities also necessitates extra work. A pivot table can become extremely helpful in these situations since it just requires a few minutes to analyze sets of data using one.

Consider the following scenario: you have a dataset of regions and revenue numbers. You might be interested in knowing the amount of revenues per country that can be used to assess whether a region is underperforming and how to develop in that market. You can quickly generate a report in Excel using a pivot table and store it for future review.

In Excel, a Pivot Table helps you summarize data as estimates, sums, or counts from data in another Spreadsheet or table. Since you can filter and visualize data efficiently, it's ideal for quickly creating data.

For example, if you're doing data analysis, you might have created a spreadsheet that you can copy and paste into MS Excel, or use that in Google Docs and if you prefer (just go to File >Make a Copy).

The spreadsheet includes details from a fake company's consumer purchases. Since businesses spend at various times, we'll use a pivot table to consolidate this Data so we can see overall sales by business and evaluate transactions through companies for fast analysis.

The Pivot table helps you rearrange a table containing tons of details so that you can see the information that applies to you.

A. You may pick the whole dataset you like to look at it and choose: "Data" -> "PivotTable" on either a Mac or even a PC. When you click that, a new tab with a table should open.

B. Drag and remove the Row Labels, Column Labels, and Report Filter until you have the table next to you.

- The top row of the table should have column labels (for example, Month, Date, Company Name)
- Row Labels run down the left side of the table [for example, Month, Date, and Company Name (as with column labels, that depends on whether you choose to view the Data horizontally and vertically)]
- The data to be measured should be entered in the Values section (for example, Revenue, Purchases)
- Report Filter aids in the refinement of the performance. Fill in the blanks of anything you'd like to filter through (For instance, you might want to check at Lead Referral Sources but leave Google and Direct out.)

Pivot tables are a fantastic way to keep track of the details in the reports. You may copy and paste data into your Excel file or use Google Apps to make a copy (File >Make a Copy).

Analyzing Data Sets with Excel

You can quickly generate various forms of charts, such as line & column charts, or incorporate miniature diagrams if you know how to interpret data in Excel. You may also use conditional formatting, add a table design, build PivotTables, easily insert totals, or apply a table style. If you obey a few basic guidelines, analyzing massive data sets using Excel becomes a lot easier:

- Choose the cells that store the information you want to examine.

- Click the Quick Analysis key image button (or press CRTL +Q) that appears to bottom right of the selected results.
- The Quick Analysis Lens button is visible on selected data.
- Pick a tab from the gallery of Quick Analysis. Choose Charts, for example, to see the data in a chart.
- Choose one of the options, or point to each to see a preview.
- You'll find that the options available to you aren't all the same. This is due to the fact that the choices vary depending on the kind of data you've chosen in your workbook.

To learn the suitable method to analyze data in Excel, you'll need to recognize that the analysis approach is appropriate for you.

1. Formatting: Formatting allows you to draw attention to certain aspects of the data using data bars & colors. This, among other aspects, allows you to easily see high or low values.
2. Charts: Charts Excel suggests various charts depending on the kind of data you've selected.
3. Totals: Totals enable you to add and subtract numbers from rows or columns. Running Total, for example, inserts a total that expands when you add things to the results. Additional alternatives can be seen by clicking the small black arrows on right & left.
4. Tables: Tables make filtering and sorting data. Click More if you don't see table style you want.
5. Sparklines: Sparklines are small graphs that can be shown alongside data. They enable you to see trends quickly.

Tips and Tricks

If you play your cards correctly, data analysis in MS Excel can be a lot of fun. We've compiled a list of short tips to help you understand how to analyze data in Excel.

Cleaning of data

With a few tips & techniques, one of the most common Excel functions. You will learn how to use the native Excel function and how to use Power Query to achieve the same aim. Excel 2016 has a built-in function called Power Query, and Excel 2010/2013 has an Add-in called Power Query. With just only a few clicks, you can actually import, convert, and load your data.

Change the number format from text to numeric.

When you upload data from a source other than MS Excel, numbers are often converted to text. Excel can notify you by displaying a green tooltip in cell's top-left corner.

You can easily convert values to numbers by tapping on 'Convert to number' inside the tooltip choices, depending on number of values in range.

If you actually have more than 1000 values, you may have to wait a few seconds for Excel to complete the conversion.

You may also use Text-to-Columns to translate values to number format by following these steps:

1. Choose the set of values that need to be converted.
2. Choose Data >Text to Columns from the menu bar.
3. Click Next after selecting Delimited.
4. Uncheck both of the delimiter checkboxes (see below) and press Next.
5. Text-Columns-Checkboxes

6. Click Finish after selecting General.

When you have a large amount of numbers to convert, such trick will save you time over waiting for all of them to be converted. Simply right-click on column header of column you wish to convert in Power Query.

1. Choose Change Type.
2. Next, choose the number type you like (such as Whole Number or Decimal)
3. Power-Query-Data-Type

Data Analysis

Excel analytics makes data analysis easier and quicker. Here are few work-related suggestions:

1. Using Excel Tables to build auto-expandable ranges: Excel Tables are one of the most underutilized aspects of MS Excel. Excel Tables have a lot of great features that let you function faster. The following are some of these characteristics:
2. Formula Auto Fill: As you insert a formula in the table, it will automatically be copied to the table's remainder.
3. Auto Expansion: New objects typed below or to the right of table are added to the table automatically.
4. Visible headers: The headers will still be visible, regardless of where you are in the table.
5. Automatic Total Row: To evaluate total of a row, pick the formula you want to use.

6. Use Excel Tables in a Formula: Much like dropdown lists, whenever you have formula that relies on a Table, the relation in the formula would be automatically changed when new objects are added to the Table.

7. Using Excel Tables as a Chart Source: Once you use an MS Excel Table as a chart source, the chart would be automatically changed. As you can see, the Excel Tables let you build databases that don't need to be changed any time new information is added.

Data Visualization

Quickly visualize trends: Sparklines are a Microsoft Excel visualization feature that helps you quickly visualize general pattern of a set of values. Sparklines are mini-graphs that appear inside cells. You would want to imagine the average pattern of a collective of salesmen's monthly sales.

Follow the measures below to make the sparklines:

1. Choose the set that includes the Data you'll be plotting (This move is suggested but not required; you can choose your data set later.)

2. Choose Sparklines from the Insert menu. Choose from three types of sparklines: line, column, or win/loss.

3. Pick a list by clicking the range selection icon. Choose a Selection to find the position of the sparklines, use the Excel Button, press Enter, and then click OK. Ensure that the position you use is relative to the data source. For, e.g., if data source range has 6 rows, the sparkline's position must also have 6 rows.

You will use the following to format the sparkline:

To adjust the color of markers, do the following:

1. To reach the Sparkline Tools menu, click on cell inside the sparkline.

2. Go to Marker Color in Sparkline tools menu and adjust the color for the individual markers you like.

For instance, high points go on green, low points go on the red, and the rest goes on the blue.

To alter the line width, use the following commands:

1. To access the Sparkline Tools menu, click a cell inside the sparkline.
2. Go to Sparkline Color >Weight in Sparkline Tools contextual menu and adjust the line width as required.

Save your time with Quick Analysis: The Quick Analysis function was one of the considerable enhancements in Excel 2021. By simply pressing an actual button, you can easily generate graphs, sparklines, PivotCharts, PivotTables, and summary functions.

When you pick data in MS Excel 2013 or later, the Fast Analysis Excel Button appears in bottom-right corner of the set you've chosen. The following choices will appear when you press the Fast Analysis button:

1. Charts
2. Formatting
3. Totals
4. Sparklines
5. Tables

When you choose one of the tools, Excel will show a summary of the potential outcomes based on the Data you entered.

1. If you go to charts and press the Quick Analysis tab, you will easily generate the graph below by simply pressing a button.

2. You can easily insert a row with average by each column if you go to Totals:

3. You can easily attach Sparklines by clicking on Sparklines tab:

4. As you can see, that Quick Analysis function helps you conduct various visualizations and analyses efficiently and with little effort.

Data Reporting

Data reporting in Excel analytics necessitates more than just accounting skills; it often necessitates a detailed understanding of Excel functionalities as well as the ability to make the report visually appealing.

1. Before updating the Excel workbook, disable Auto Refresh. When you make modifications to the worksheet, this would prevent the table from updating. To do so, tap "Switch auto-refresh off" from the Refresh icon at bottom of Excel Report Designer Task-Pane.

2. Pick a cell in table region below where you'd like to place the new row while inserting a new row to layout. Then right-click and choose Insert >Table Rows Above from the context menu.

3. Using the Table Delete functions equivalent to the Insert functions to delete columns or rows. Click a cell in table region of the column or row you wish to delete to remove it. Then right-click and actually choose Delete from the context menu, followed by Table Columns & Table Rows.

4. Exclude any rows or columns that aren't required from the graph. It's simpler for the table to reload if fewer cells are in the arrangement, so deleting those that aren't required would increase results.

There are also other uses for Excel that might not have been included here. To learn about the infinite range of functions available in Excel analytics, experiment with visualizing abstract details or organizing disparate numbers. If you want to work in data processing, having a solid understanding of Excel is a must.

The Importance of Reporting All Results

It is essential to disclose all results, even though they are negligible while evaluating data. It's also crucial to avoid grouping data analyses together and to make broad generalizations. A researcher reporting on the efficacy of visual aid in increasing awareness of cataracts, for example, gives patients a 10-question survey before and after giving them the visual aid. The visual assistance, according to the report, improves the average amount of correctly answered questions. It is a decent beginning, but it is insufficient. The researcher must carefully examine the findings of each particular query. Knowing that the technique improves general comprehension offers no insight on the intervention's benefits and disadvantages. Maybe the initiative increased the number of people who know what the cataract is, but maybe not the number of people who know how to properly treat a cataract. It is crucial to know since it allows the action to be tweaked to help communicate the required detail.

This knowledge acquisition analyzes data in Excel and how to analyze revenue data in Excel, and a few data analysis examples.

PowerPoint

The PowerPoint program, offered by the Office package, is one of those tools that nowadays one cannot not be familiar with, whether in school, university or work. In this book we will find out what Power Point is, what it is used for and how to use it in its main features. As we mentioned, the Power Point program is part of the actual Microsoft Office package and is used for creating presentations of content through multimedia slides. Do you know the old slides that were transmitted via projector? Here with Power Point you can create, edit, animate all the slides that will make up a final presentation. Thanks to its many features Power Point is a widely used program in both business and studies, starting as early as high school. In fact, for a long time students engaged in group work have been required to use Power Point to show the fruit of their work, not to mention the possibility it offers to clearly set up the term paper to be used during high school exams. The same is true in the university environment, where the use of Power Point can start from lectures and go all the way up to the presentation of one's final paper in the graduation session.

To use Power Point you must first install the program on your PC.

Introduction to Microsoft PowerPoint

What is PowerPoint?

PowerPoint is presentation software that enables users to create slideshows with critical data, graphs, and images. These slideshows can be used to present information to an audience in an effective way. PowerPoint is a versatile tool with many features that can be exploited to create more sophisticated presentations.

However, users ought to take the time to fully absorb how to use all the features to reap the full benefits. If you know how to do something quickly and efficiently, you will be able to save time and be more productive. Most PowerPoint presentations are created using a template, which includes specifying a background color or image, choosing a standard font, and selecting from a range of slide layouts. This makes it easy to create consistent, professional-looking presentations.

The changes you make to the template can be saved as a "master slide" to be used as a starting point for future presentations. When the master slide is changed, for example, by choosing a new background image, those changes will be applied to all the other slides in the presentation. This helps to ensure that the slides in the presentation have a consistent appearance.

Why Use and Learn Microsoft PowerPoint

Microsoft PowerPoint is a software tool that can be used to create presentations. This app has several features that facilitate communication. PowerPoint slides can be customized to your specific needs and contents. This lets you tailor your presentation to your audience and ensure that the information you present is relevant and engaging.

Using specific, targeted slide decks makes them more versatile and helpful than generic slide decks. Adding images, audio, video, and animations is beneficial and makes your presentation more attractive. Using these tools will help you be more spontaneous and engage more effectively with your audience. PowerPoint has various features that can assist in making complex information more understandable and manageable. This can be accomplished by utilizing features such as tables and SmartArt. PowerPoint's review features allow for comments and notes, making collaboration easy.

You can share your PowerPoint presentation with anyone, anywhere, and even on YouTube without losing any of its formatting. PowerPoint is an important learning tool for business professionals who need it to stay competitive. PowerPoint presentations make a great impression with their well-crafted structure and striking visuals. This powerful application can help your presentations stand out from the crowd. PowerPoint can be an excellent tool for engagingly communicating your ideas and stories. You can create visually stunning and easy-to-understand slides with a few simple tools.

This makes it easy to share your ideas with others, and they will be able to understand them easily. PowerPoint makes it easy to share your ideas with a large audience. Whether planning a presentation for work or a special occasion, PowerPoint can help create an unforgettable experience for your audience. Guest posting PowerPoint can help you to communicate effectively with your readers by using built-in themes, animation features, and a polished presentation style. PowerPoint is a high-quality tool for use by professionals.

Presentations are a great way to communicate your ideas to a group. This can help get your message across to a large audience. Using attractive presentation templates and graphics can make a great impression on your job.

Creating a New Presentation

Preparing presentations might be a big part of your daily activities. Although there are presently several tools available to do so, using Microsoft PowerPoint is still many people's preferred method. Whether it is a personal or business presentation, this tool still provides the most resources for such. Let's take an actual look at some of the main features of the software and how it can be used. As mentioned earlier, some of the formatting and inserting tools that it presents are similar to Excel and Word and, therefore, if you have any doubts.

Creating a Presentation

When you open a new file in Powerpoint, the program will automatically open a blank slide that allows you to add a title and a subtitle. This will be the beginning of a presentation where you will style yourself with the necessary images, text, and any other resource you might want. The initial layout that you will see on the page is pretty simple: There is a slide with the options in the center of the screen and a scroll bar to the left where you can see all the slides your presentation contains.

If you wish to add new slides, you have three options:

1. Click on new slide on the slides section of the ribbon in the home tab.
2. Click on new slide on the slides button of the insert tab of the ribbon.
3. Click on the slide thumbnail panel (to the left) of the presentation with the right button and select new slide.

When you add a new slide, it will automatically bring you a predefined one with a place to add the titles and to add text. Use the text formatting tools in the ribbon home tab to style them accordingly.

Suppose, however, that you do not like the layout of the slide and would like to change it. PowerPoint allows two ways to change this design: The first is by clicking on the layout button under the slides section in the home tab. The other is to click with the right button of your mouse on the window that has the slide you want to change and selecting layout. If you apply a style, which you will read more about in the next section of this chapter, the software will provide you with several different layouts. If there is no style applied, Powerpoint will just present you with different boxes to apply the format you wish.

Pro tip: Add new slides to the middle of your presentation or any other place you deem necessary, by clicking on the place you want to insert it in the thumbnail panel. A red line should appear between the slides, and all you need to do is select the right button of the mouse and click on new slide.

Moving Things Around

Managing the slides in Excel is easier than you might imagine—it is all done through the thumbnail panel on your screen's left side. First, you need to know that this panel is designed to scroll up and down so you can see what slides compose your presentation. This being said, if you want to move a slide, all you need to do is click on the selected one and move it through the different slides that will appear by dragging and dropping. This will make your management of the presentation easier, and you do not need to worry about deleting or starting over.

To delete a slide, the process is almost the same. You should go to the thumbnail panel and click the right button on the slide you wish to delete. A menu will appear, from which you will select delete slide. Another option is to select the slide and press the delete button on your keyboard. If you have mistakenly done so, do not worry. You can bring it back by using the undo function available on the ribbon or use the undo shortcut on your keyboard.

Pro tip: When you open a PowerPoint template, you will see that there is a dotted line within the slide. This line will not appear in your presentation. Rather, it is used to delimit the area to which you will add the text, the images, or whatever other content you decide. You can actually increase or decrease the size of this work area by clicking on the line and dragging it to reach the size that you wish to achieve. To add a dialogue box to add text, all you need to actually do is click on the text box button in the text section of the actual insert tab of the ribbon.

Applying Themes

Sometimes companies have a template that they offer to all the employees to use in their presentations. However, if this is not your case, you do not need to worry: PowerPoint offers its users the possibility of applying one of its available themes and templates for cases like these. Keep reading to find out what the differences are between them and how to decide which one is best for your presentation.

Themes

When you decide to start a presentation, you can choose to apply a theme to it. This means that PowerPoint will provide a predetermined set of fonts, colors, styles, and visual effects for your presentation. These possibilities are available in the design tab of the ribbon, under the themes section. There, you will find several standard styles you can apply to your presentation and their potential variations.

While the program already comes with some options, you can also look for others on the internet by using the search feature by clicking on the down arrow to the right side of the theme box. As you add new slides, you will see that they will keep the established formatting. However, do not worry if you want to change the layout and are afraid of making changes. If you follow one of the steps mentioned above to add a new layout, the program will automatically offer you already formatted layout options for you to select from.

Essentially, using a theme will be applicable when you already have an idea of what you want to put in your presentation, and you do not need any orientation on what and how to add. It will allow you to creatively and freely add your ideas to it by only establishing a standardized format to it. Differently than with the template function, using the theme tool will give you some direction while allowing you to establish the flow of the presentation.

Templates

The templates in PowerPoint are available in the file tab of the document. The software shows the user several options and allows you to choose from one online. Be aware that these are not determined for each situation that the user might want but rather more what you want the presentation to look like. Be advised that while some of these themes may present over 20 slide options to choose from, others have fewer options. It is also important to state that some of these styles will bring you a defined outline for the presentation. You do not necessarily need to stick to them, and you can change them according to your needs.

Adding and Formatting Slides

Changing the Layout of Your Slide

Sometimes, you just may not like the layout of your slides. How can you get them touched up? What do you do when halfway into filling your slide; Do you realize that your content needs to be set within two content panes? Follow the steps below to get through that.

1. Click the thumbnail meant for the slide you want to refine. If you want to deal with all of the slides, click the thumbnails of slides.

2. Click the Layout feature in the Slides group within the Home panel. You would then see all the layout styles you can use for your slides.

3. Click the new layout you want to work with. Instantly, the previous layout for the slide changes to whatever new layout you click.

4. Sometimes, the contents appear haphazard and out of line after changing the layout of your slide(s). This is where you'll need to do a little editing, resizing, and shifting.

Fashioning a Look for Your Presentation

Presentations should always be catching and visually appealing. Here, we will look at how you can achieve all of that. First, let's see how you can change the color of your text box from the default white color. You'd be working with the Shape Fill tool for this, though. After clicking that, you can choose from the range of colors on your screen. There's another tool you should be aware of—the Eyedropper tool. It works to copy the color of an object on a slide to the shape's outline. Below are the procedures that describe how you can work with the tool;

1. Click the shape on the slide you want to color, and then click the Shape Outline feature on the panel.

2. You'd be directed to a gallery for the Shape Outline feature. Click the Eyedropper tool.

3. Use your mouse to drag the tool to the object that bears the color you want to use. The moment you click that color, your text box or slide gets filled with the color too.

The next feature you need to consider is the Format icon within the Format Shape panel. There, you have access to several tools and effects, all of which are described below;

- **Shadow:** This feature gives your text box a Shade effect. You can reduce or increase the shadow effect applied to your text box. This tool also embraces other features that control your text box or slide's transparency, size, blur, angle, and distance.

- **Reflection:** This feature also deals with some of the abovementioned features—transparency, distance, size, and blur. The only difference is that this feature controls how reflective the test box appears.

- **Glow:** This feature allows the ends of the text box or slide to glow. The features that regulate the glow include—color, size, and transparency.

- **Soft edges:** This tool allows you to work on the soft edges of your text box. These tools can also control soft edges, transparency, glow, color, size, etc.

- **3D format:** This tool allows you to apply a specific three-dimensional effect to your text box. The tools for this feature include Contour, Depth, Bevel, Material, Lighting, etc. For the bevel feature, you can work with the gallery of choices. You can also adjust the contour and depth of your text box by selecting one color and using the adjacent spin box for controls.

- **3D rotation:** This tool allows you to flip a three-dimensional version of your textbox while working with functions peculiar to each axis.

If you have a table within your presentation, you can also change the layout to make your presentation more beautiful. Here are some of the features that you can work with, as well as their functions.

- **Table:** This feature allows you to adjust the gridlines of your table. The Select feature can highlight columns, rows, or the entire table. The tools present within this feature include the special feature, the view gridlines feature, etc.

- **Rows and Columns:** This feature allows you to access tools that fix rows and columns into a table. When inserting rows and columns, you can insert them to either the left or right side of your table. The Delete feature can cut out certain rows and columns from the table.

- **Merge:** The cells in your table can be joined by their edges, so they come off as one. The feature you need for this is the Merge Cells feature. To separate two merged cells, work with the Split Cells feature. If you want a cell to split into more than two cells, you can specify that within the dialog box for split cells.
- **Cell size:** This feature is what you work with when you need to change the width or height of a row or column in your table. The spin boxes for these parameters allow for the altering of the dimensions. You could also work with the Distribute feature, which allows you to create even numbers of rows and columns. If you use both the Distribute Rows and Distribute Columns features simultaneously, the cells in the tables would become uniform.
- **Alignment:** This feature is what you need when you have to align the text in your slides. Alignment can be either to the cells' right or left. If you want the text you be aligned vertically, click the Align Top feature. You can also use this feature to incline the text on tables in different directions.
- **Table size:** This feature allows you to control the table size in your slide. Note that while controlling the table size, the height and width may grow out of uniformity. If you want to prevent that from happening, click the Lock Aspect Ratio checkbox.
- **Arrange:** This feature allows you to determine the direction in which the tables, text boxes, shapes, etc., are set on a slide. For example, you could decide to send certain items backward or forward.

Inserting Images, Videos, and Other Media

While preparing a presentation, you might need to add a picture, an icon, or even a video to illustrate the point you want to make. This is not a problem for the users of PowerPoint software since it enables users to add several different types of objects within the presentation and make them interactive while presenting. For the newer versions of Powerpoint, if you open a new slide apart from the first one, you will see eight small icons available in the text box from which you can choose. They comprise a table, a graph, a form, a 3D object, pictures, online pictures, or an icon.

Inserting Pictures

Inserting a picture into a presentation can be as easy as using the copy and paste options, the keyboard shortcuts, or the options in the ribbon. When you add an image, PowerPoint will enable you to choose a file from your computer or online.

The same process applies to adding shapes or SmartArt. Remember that these will initially be placed within the work area of the slide. To resize them and have them auto-adjust, increase the work area or click on the image to drag and resize it, using the shift button to maintain its proportions.

Another option that the software gives the user is the possibility to add a photo album to a determined slide. These can be used in cases for which you will need to illustrate the slide with more than one picture, and you don't want to show them all at once. The option to insert one of these albums is available in the images section of the insert tab.

When you click on the button, a dialogue box will open for you to decide what pictures you want to add. In this case, they will need to be stored on your computer so that the program can find them. To search for these images, go to the file/disk option to look for them. You can actually add as many as you want depending on the specific size you want your presentation to have. There will also be the option as to how you want to fit the images to the slide, if you want to add captions, and the shape that you want the album to have.

Once the album is added, it will appear in the selected slide. To make the pictures appear and change during the presentation, you will need to click on it or press enter. These image features will enable you to make your presentation friendlier and free of so much text, capturing the attention of those participating and bringing a colorful element to the picture.

Inserting Videos and Sound

Inserting video and sound into your presentation may seem hard, but doing so is, in fact, pretty easy. For videos, you can add either online videos without the need to download them to your computer, or you can add a video that you have stored on your hard drive. As for sound, these will need to be stored on your computer so that it can be uploaded when you select it.

Let's start with adding videos, which is an incredible feature to bring more liveliness to your presentation. For these cases, you cannot use the copy and paste feature. Instead, you will need to use the insert video feature in the insert tab's media section. Once you click on the down-pointing arrow, it will ask you if you want to upload a video from your device or if you want to use an online source. If you use a media feature stored on your computer, the process will be similar to adding a picture.

However, if your option is to source the video directly from the internet, you can do so by using several platforms: YouTube, Vimeo, SlideShare, Stream, and Flip. These are the only platforms supported by the software, so they will be the only ones you can choose from. You will need to search for the video in your usual browser in one of the supported channels. Once you have found it, copy the address that appears in the navigation bar of your browser and paste it into the field with a magnifying glass in PowerPoint that opens when you click add online video. You will be able to preview the video before adding it. Just click on enter, and it will appear in the selected slide.

A play button will appear to play the video in both the presentation and editing modes of the presentation. You will also be able to determine the features that you want to apply to the video by clicking on it and noticing that the ribbon will change with an additional bar that says video tools. Use this bar to change its borders, apply corrections to the images, and establish effects.

A similar process will be used to add sound. The button to add these media files is next to the video button in the insert tab. The options available are to add audio from your computer files or choose a file using record and audio from your device. However, to record your voice directly into the presentation, you will need to have the recording device connected and recognized by the software for it to accept the function.

Inserting Charts

Inserting charts and graphs into a presentation is simple, and it is similar to adding one of these in Word. You will select the chart or graph that you wish to add, and the chart and an Excel file will open for you to add the data. Once the data is added, you can close the Excel window, and the chart will automatically refresh and update with the information you have added. For this feature, in case your graph is in Excel, you can also choose to copy and paste it to the presentation so that you do not need to type in all of the information again.

Pro tip: When you copy and paste a graph from another program to Word or PowerPoint, you can paste it as a picture or as an interactive feature. The toolbox that appears immediately to the side of the graph once it is pasted will give you several options on how you want to paste it—as a picture, with links, or as a simple object. If you decide to paste it as a picture, the elements will not move and will remain the same. However, if you paste it with links, every time you modify the origin file, the chart will be modified as well, needing both of the programs to be opened so that the information can be updated once it is done.

Delivering a Powerful Presentation

When delivering a presentation, you must employ several strategies to ensure that your audience gets the message you are trying to convey. These strategies would require you to do a lot of planning and studying. Let's see some things you should consider first;

- **Your audience:** You must know the people you'd deliver your content to. This knowledge would help you decide on the tone and style you use for your presentation. For example, presenting an idea to kids requires that you work with funny and engaging effects. You also wouldn't want to use jargon that your audience may not be familiar with. And if you have to use terms they may not be familiar with, ensure that you set routes to help them understand the message you are trying to convey. This is where video inserts will help.

- **Purpose:** Understanding the aim or target your presentation is aimed at will help you gather relatable content within your presentation. For example, a presentation aimed at changing your audience's mindset regarding a particular belief should contain so many facts and content that will make them agree with you. You should also employ the same technique to convince your audience to invest in your idea. Make them understand why they have to buy into it. Work with as many convincing details as possible. You should also have a slide dedicated to your concluding point or idea.

- **Place:** Knowing where to deliver your presentation beforehand will also do a lot of good in ensuring that the presentation goes smoothly. For example, if your presentation contains many links to the Internet, you want to ensure that the location has a stable Internet connection. You should always go out with your laptops and not just flash drives. The location may not have an excellent laptop to anchor your presentation with. The last things you should prepare are hardcopies of your presentation. That way, you can go on without any hitch if there's any issue.

You must also pay attention to some commands when working with a slideshow. Here, a total of six tools will be listed. They include the following;

1. **Previous:** This tool takes you to the former slide, i.e., the one before the current slide. You might need to reiterate something you said or reference a previously highlighted detail during your presentation.

2. **Next:** This tool takes you to the slide that comes after your current slide.

3. **Pointer gallery:** While running through your presentation, you may need to draw something against your slides to make an illustration or a more detailed description. This gallery lets you switch the mouse pointer to pens, erasers, or highlighters.

4. **See All Slides View:** With this feature, you get access to all the thumbnails of your slides. This feature allows you to jump right into any slide without working with the 'next' or 'previous' parts.

5. **Zoom:** This feature allows you to enlarge a particular area or section of your slide. A double tap will zoom into your slide if you are working with your laptop.

6. **Subtitles:** With this feature, you can activate or deactivate features like subtitles, captions, etc.

7. **Menu:** This feature is what you need when accessing some tools. Some tools include 'Return to the previously viewed slide,' 'End Show,' etc.

OneNote

Introduction to Microsoft OneNote

OneNote is one of Microsoft's historic applications. Initially distributed as part of the Office package, OneNote has morphed into a program rooted in the cloud that allows note-taking from any device, from a traditional desktop system as well as from a tablet or smartphone. A free version of OneNote was distributed in mid-2010, but only recently has Microsoft taken the plunge by removing all the limitations present in the free release.

What is OneNote and How It Works?

OneNote is an application designed for note-taking and note-taking, a tool that allows you to collect a lot of information from different sources in one place. One can write text of one's own or retrieve information posted on the web, with even the ability to cut out Internet pages.

The program also contains convenient OCR that allows for optical character recognition, so simply submit a photo of a text or scan of a document to OneNote to turn the image content into editable text. In OneNote, notes are organized as tabs which, in turn, can contain one or more pages. All tabs are part of a single clipboard: OneNote allows management of more than one clipboard.

The additional icon located in the Windows taskbar allows you to quickly create a new note in OneNote (New Quick Note); send content to OneNote, whatever kind it is (Send to OneNote); crop a portion of a web page that you are interested in (Screen Crop). With the release of the new, free version of OneNote, Microsoft has eliminated all of the restrictions that previously made the software less feature-rich and flexible than the version included with the Office suite. Free OneNote is identical to the version included in Office, except that it can only be used with OneDrive. Because of this, OneDrive, the Microsoft-branded cloud storage service, is where all of your notebooks will live permanently. You'll have to accept relying solely on OneDrive for note storage, as local storage won't be an option. The benefit of using OneNote, however, is that all of your notes will be accessible and editable from any computer, laptop, tablet, smartphone, etc., regardless of the operating system.

Main Features

Even if a recipient does not have OneNote, you can still share your notes with them. To make a new notepad, for instance, go to File, New, and then click the Create Notepad button. If you want other users to take action on the notes' content and provide input, you can invite them by clicking Invite Users and entering their e-mail address. The web-based version of OneNote, known as OneNote Online, is a reliable alternative for those who do not have the desktop application.

Indeed, we advise users who install the OneNote app to sign in with OneNote Online notwithstanding to see how each note may be changed from the web by joining in with their Microsoft user account. With the OneNote app for Android and iOS, you can take notes on the go. After creating notes in OneNote on a desktop or laptop computer, they may be accessed and edited on the go by downloading the corresponding app for their smartphone and signing in with their Microsoft account. You can instantly save a picture of a document by clicking on the icon displaying a miniature camera from a mobile device. Once the image has been captured and uploaded to the OneDrive servers, it will become an integral component of the selected note and will be accessible from any device running OneNote. Right-clicking the image in OneNote and choosing "Copy Text from Image" will OCR (optical character recognition) the complete contents of the image.

The free version of OneNote now allows you to protect tabs containing personal information using a password. To proceed, simply right-click on the tab name then choose Protect section with password.

Another new feature for the free version of OneNote is support for audio/video recording. Indeed, from now on, the Insert menu's Record Audio and Record Video buttons will allow you to add audio and video comments, respectively. Last but not least, the new Page Versions button in the History menu lets you "browse" through different iterations of the same tab. Thus, among the main functions of this software we can mention:

Synchronization between different devices

For mobile devices there are respective apps. This way you can easily retrieve your content from smartphones and tablets and also add new content. Different devices will always be synchronized and so you will not lose any notes.

Collaboration with other users

If you need to share a content with other people, you can create a specific block and invite your collaborators via e-mail.

Integration with other Office tools

OneNote is a Microsoft product, so it is natural for its developers to create synergies with the parent company's other tools such as Outlook's calendars and to-do lists, Memo notes, and Excel spreadsheets.

Creating a New Notebook

Once you launch OneNote, it will ask you if you want to create a new notebook or open an existing one. Suppose that we want to start a new one—the first thing that needs to be done is give it a name. As soon as the name is determined, the program will open to a blank page with the ribbon omitted. The first thing you might actually want to do is click on the home tab of the ribbon, expand it, and pin it to the top of the table.

Although we have already seen this in the first chapter, let's recap: After you expand the ribbon, to pin it to the window, click on the thumbnail located to the far right of the task pane.

As you will notice from viewing the ribbon for the first time, it is again similar to other programs in the Microsoft Suite, making it much easier to navigate. In OneNote, you will have the usual font formatting tools, the option of pasting and cutting, and using bullet points or numbered lists. Other features that are the same include the review pane, that offers the user with translation and spellcheck possibilities.

When your first notebook is open, you will see that it has a color and that there is a line for you to type in the name of the page. This page will be inside a section, which is what this color tab means. To rename the section according to your needs, double-click on the name and type the label that is relevant to you. In this case, if you are preparing a kitchen notebook, you might want to type in recipes.

On the first line that appears on the page, you will write the title of this page. Maintaining our example, you can put the name of a dish in the title. To add more pages to this section of the notebook—and you can add as many as you wish—click on the top of the pane to the right of your screen where it says add page. By clicking on this button, you will add pages to the relevant section.

Pro tip: There is no need to worry about renaming the pages since this will be done automatically by one note when you type in the title of the page on the first line that is there.

Creating and Editing Sections and Pages

Now, let's say that you want to add more than recipes to this notebook, but you do not want the pages to be mixed. You can do this by creating another section. To create a new section, click on the + button that is next to the first color coded tab. This will automatically create a new section, and the color will be established for you. However, if you do not feel this is the right one, or you want to change it, you can click on top of the tab with the right button and establish the color of your preference.

By clicking on the right button, you will also be able to delete the created section, export, or create a new section group. If you choose to create a new group, this will allow you to place all of the sections related to a certain area to it. At first, we were creating a notebook for the kitchen, but let's say that you want to have one to place all of your home information.

You can create different groups with the different areas of the house and place the distinct sections pertaining to it within the group. This will appear on top of the canvas as a new section group. You will be able to rename it by clicking on the right button as well.

Using Templates and Other Formats

Sometimes you might want to apply a specific format to the page that you are creating. This can be a to-do list, maybe some lecture notes, or an index card. OneNote has a specific feature for this, allowing you to use one of the templates that have been pre-established to meet your needs. To find the available templates, you will need to go to the insert tab on the ribbon and click on the page templates button under the pages section. The software will actually allow you to choose between several options and, once you click on your selection, the page will be automatically updated.

If you would rather edit the format by yourself, you will have the option to add a spreadsheet, a picture, a video, a table, or even equations, symbols, and stickers. All of these options are available on the insert tab of the ribbon in their relevant sections. Some of these options allow you to work inside them, such as the Excel spreadsheet and the table. Others, such as the stickers, are used only for decoration and cannot be edited within the canvas areas.

Pro tip: If you add a picture with a text to the canvas area you might not initially be able to edit it. However, OneNote has a feature that will enable you to extract the information from the image and edit it. To start, copy and paste the image to the work area. Once you have done this, click on the image with the right button and select the copy text from picture option. Click on another area of the canvas, and the extracted text will be placed there for you to edit accordingly.

Page Settings

If you want to edit your page and, for example, omit its title or add lines to the canvas, this is not only possible, but a whole section in the ribbon is dedicated to it. Under the view tab of the ribbon under the page setup section, you can actually change the page's color, add rule lines to it (there are several options to select from), and even hide the page title. In the button named switch background, you will be able to actually change the color of the canvas to dark mode, which some users commonly prefer.

Now, suppose that you have the intention of printing these notes or some sections of the notebook. You can adjust the paper format so that you do not write out of the printing area. To select the size of the paper that you want to see, go to the paper size button.

Once you click on it, a pane will appear to the side of your window. In it, you will be able to choose the size paper you want to use, its orientation (landscape or portrait), and if it should have any margins.

At the bottom of the options, you will see a checkbox that will enable you to determine if your selection is supposed to be a template or not. If you want it to be, you will need to determine a name before saving. Another thing that OneNote will allow you to do is establish if this page format should be the standard for all the pages in the section.

Adding and Organizing Notes

After you have determined the title for the page, you can start writing down your notes. While a normal text is applicable to the pages, you might want to use some of the tags to make your document more user-friendly. In the home tab of the ribbon, you will find all the quick formats for the text as well as their keyboard shortcut in parenthesis. Among the options are the possibility to write to-do checkboxes, icons for passwords, addresses, telephones, and options to highlight your text.

When you click to select any one of these, they will appear at the last place where your cursor was located in the canvas, but you will be able to move them around. By clicking and dragging each of the options, you can place them where you think it is more appropriate. Since this is a free space for your creations, you can place them where you feel is the best place.

Once you select the icon, a box will appear around it. Click on the ellipsis at the top to see more quick options for formatting the text and making modifications. You can also use the movement arrow to resize the dialogue box and make it the size you desire. To eliminate the quick tag you have created, you can select it and press delete, or you can also click on the X button in the basic text section of the home tab.

Searching for Tags

OneNote will allow you to search your notebooks for any potential tags that you might want to find. To do this, you must go to the find tags button on the tags section of the home tab. Once you click on it, a pane will appear on your screen that will allow you to search for the tags by name, section, title, date, or note text. A list of possible tags will appear, and you can choose from it.

Unless otherwise selected, the program will automatically search for all of the related tags within the mentioned notebook. However, this information can be changed on the bottom of the tags summary pane. Here you can choose between searching parts, such as the notebook, sections, and pages, or you can choose to search by time of creation, such as tags created in the past week or yesterday's notes.

Finally, if you want to have an editable list of all the tags you have created in one of your notebook pages, this is also possible. First, you will need to select on what page you want to place the list. Next, go to the tags summary pane and select the create summary page button to have a list of all the tags within the selected area added to this page. Once again, you will need to specify the information of when or where you want the tags to be from.

Customizing Tags

If you feel like the tags that are available are not the right fit for your project, you can customize and create your own. To do this, go to the find tags button on the home pane and click on it. At the bottom of the pane, you will see the option to customize tags. Click on the actual link, and you will see that a dialogue box will open.

Here, you should choose between creating a new tag or modifying an existing one. If you decide to create a new tag, you can click on the button.

You will need to select a name for it, determine if there is a specific symbol you would like to use from the available list, the font color, and if you want it to be highlighted or not. A window at the bottom of this dialogue box will show you a preview of what your tag will look like. Once you are satisfied with the result, click on ok, and the tag will be automatically created for you.

Creating Links

One of the best parts of OneNote is that you can create a link from one section to the other. This is enabled by the create links section that appears when you click on the mouse's right button. The first thing you actually need to do is select the place in the canvas where you want to place the link. Next, right-click with the mouse and select the option link. Once you do, a dialogue box with all your notebooks and sections will open.

You will need to type in the text what you want to be displayed. Next, you will have two possibilities. The first is to choose a document or a webpage to the link. This means that you do not actually need to necessarily add a link to something that was in your notebook exclusively, rather create one to anything that is on your device or on the internet. The other option will be to add a link from another section of one of the existing notebooks.

To do this, browse through the available sections until you find the one that you are looking for. Here, you can link a page or a section from the current notebook or another notebook. This feature is only allowed because you will have all the OneNote notebooks available to you in this view. After you have selected, click on the ok button, and the link will be automatically created. Once again, use the drag and drop feature to place it where you think is relevant.

Drawing and Sketching

If you use a mobile device such as a tablet, for example, to use OneNote, you will see several advantages in drawing and sketching features. If you click on the draw tab in the ribbon, you will see that there are certain tools to help you draw on the canvas. Using a pen with your mobile device will make it especially easy to transform your hand-made designs to something you can register on OneNote.

While you can still draw shapes by adding the available ones in the shapes section, you can also manually draw them. The software will enable you to choose the thickness of the line, its color, and even if you would like some highlighting options. To erase something you have drawn, click on the eraser button, which will also allow you to choose the size you wish to use.

Pro tip: If you are manually drawing or writing something, you can use the ink to shape, to text, or to math features to digitalize them. In these instances, once you click on one of the options, a new window will open, and you can draw the shape or write the text or the equation, and the software will convert it to a digital format.

Inserting Images, Videos, and Other Media

In Microsoft Word, you can easily insert images, videos, and other media to enhance your document's appearance and content. Here are the basic steps for inserting media in a Word document:

1. **Position the cursor:** First, place the cursor in the location of the document where you want to insert the media.

2. **Insert the media:** To insert an image or video, click on the "Insert" tab in the top menu bar of Word. Then, click on "Pictures" to insert an image, or "Online Pictures" to search for an image online. Alternatively, you can also click on "Video" to insert a video into your document. You can then choose the image or video you want to insert from your computer or search online.

3. **Position and adjust the media:** Once the image or video has been inserted, you can position and adjust its size and appearance. To move the media, simply click and drag it to the desired location. To resize the media, click and drag the corners of the image or video.

4. **Add other media:** In addition to images and videos, you can also insert other types of media into your document, such as audio files or screenshots. To insert

audio, click on the "Insert" tab and then click on "Audio". To insert a screenshot, click on the "Insert" tab and then click on "Screenshot". You can then select the audio file or screenshot you want to insert.

5. **Format the media:** You can also format the media in your document by adding borders, shadows, or effects. To do this, click on the image or video and then click on the "Format" tab in the top menu bar of Word.

In summary, inserting media in a Word document is a simple process that can enhance the appearance and content of your document. By following these basic steps, you can easily insert images, videos, audio files, and screenshots into your document and adjust their appearance and size. By formatting the media, you can add additional visual appeal to your document.

Sharing Notebooks with Others

After working on your notebook, several actions can be taken to ensure you keep track of your notes. This section covers those actions you can take to keep your notebooks secure. You can decide to share your notebook, a page, or a section with others, export them, or just save them.

Sharing

If you want to share your "personal" notebook with anybody, you need to move it to OneDrive. To do this, open your "Personal" notebook, navigate to "File" and then go down to your share option. You're going to put that on OneDrive by selecting it. You could also browse for it if you don't have it listed here.

Simply name your notebook and choose "Move notebook." You will get a message saying the notebook is now syncing to the new location, so click on "OK."

Now that you have done that, you'll see that you now have all of your share options come up because you've now put it in a location where sharing is available.

Sharing with OneDrive

It is not necessary to always share the entire notebook; if you actually prefer, you can share a single page. So, if you want to share a page from your notebook, make sure you've clicked on the page that you want to share, go up to the Home tab, and you'll see you have an option here to "Email page". (The keyboard shortcut is Ctrl + Shift + E.)

It will open an Outlook email, attach the contents of that page, and then you can then select who you want to share this with and send that email off. The user receives an email that has got the name of the notebook and an open button. If they hit that, it will open up the notebook in the browser and if that user makes a change, it will sync that change and, in your notebook, you'll see the change, with a little marker indicating that it was added by the user.

Syncing and Saving

One important thing to remember when you're sharing notebooks is that there could be multiple people accessing and eventually editing a notebook at any given time. Due to this, your notebook must be synchronized to ensure data is updated immediately.

To do this, go to the File tab and ensure you are in the "Info" area. On the right-hand side, you have a button here to view sync status. This is going to show all of the notebooks that you have and whether they're synchronized and the last time they were updated.

The option automatically selected is to sync automatically whenever there are changes. So, if you've shared this notebook with five other people and they're all in this notebook making changes, any changes they make are automatically synchronized so that you can see them.

However, if you prefer to sync manually, you have that option as well. As soon as you choose to sync manually, an "x" is placed over the notebooks to let you know that they're not currently automatically syncing.

So, if you click "Sync Now", the icon is going to change and any updates made since the last sync will be updated. If you have a lot of notebooks in here, to make this easier, you have a single button at the top as well, to "Sync All".

Password Protection

Another thing that you might want to do when sharing your notebooks is password-protect sections of them. This prevents unauthorized access to specific sections that you don't want people to see. If you want people to actually be able to see everything that's in one section but not in another section, all you need to do is right-click and select "Password protect this section."

Click "Set Password" and now, if you share this notebook, people aren't going to be able to see what's in that particular section.

To unprotect, right-click, go back into "Password protect this section", select "Remove password" and type it in to remove that protection.

Exporting Notebooks

Many of us use OneNote notebooks to organize our lives. It is important to know how to backup your OneNote because technology can fail, and when it does, you want to make sure your materials are safe and secure. Therefore, it's necessary to back up your work.

Backing up your notebook in OneNote is a great idea. There are cases where you may not have access to OneDrive, such as if you're getting a new job, you're moving to a different district, for some unforeseeable reason your server goes down, or you need access when you're not online. You need to export your OneNote.

To do this, go to your "Files" tab, and instead of choosing "Save", you're going to choose "Export". You'll get several options. You can export a page, which is handy if you just want to share a page with somebody; you can share a section; or for your own use, you can export your entire OneNote notebook. You will be able to select from a variety of file types.

You can export them as PDFs, but you can't edit them in the future. To export your OneNote as a package so that you can import it back into OneNote as its full functioning self in the future, select "OneNote Package" and then click the export button.

You're going to tell it where to save on your device, and you have your OneNote notebook saved on your hard drive for loading whatever you want, wherever you want, whether you are online or not. This can be done for group notebooks as well, so if you're in charge of your group's notebook, this is a good idea to do every once in a while, but it's also handy for individual notebooks.

Outlook

Do we not all communicate through email? Regardless of the sector in which a person works, sending and receiving emails is consistently ranked among the daily tasks that demand the highest amount of time from its participants. During the course of a typical workday, an individual devotes around 28 % of their time to checking, writing, and replying to emails (as well as looking through them). The majority of the time, emails are not managed correctly, and as a consequence, people find themselves with a cluttered inbox that just seems to become bigger as each week goes by. It is very uncommon for communications to get buried, and users may spend hours separating important and relevant information from less important information. Users of Outlook in Microsoft 365 have access to a multitude of tools that may improve the way they handle email to boost their productivity. However, to get the full advantages of these features, it is necessary to learn how to use them. If you've been looking for ways to make email more productive and less of a time suck, one option you may want to explore is switching to Microsoft Outlook. You do not need to actually open a new email account; more information on this topic may be found in the content. You can either use it from the list of Microsoft Office Desktop applications or use Outlook on the web, which essentially functions like any other email and is accessible through a web browser either on a PC or mobile and, of course, also has the mobile application that is installable on the app store of each device. It is actually available in a variety of forms. You can use it either from the list of Microsoft Office Desktop applications or use Outlook on the web. Therefore, the tools that you need to be your most productive and connected self–at home, on the road, and everywhere in between are accessible to you for your emailing life using Microsoft Outlook. These tools are available to you regardless of where you are.

Introduction to Microsoft Outlook

The Outlook 365 app is one of the apps where you have significant access to the Internet. It sends and receives your emails, schedules your meetings, keeps track of your activities daily, keeps a long list of all your contacts, etc. The good thing is that the Outlook application now has many new features.

You also get access to a vast collection of stock images. Some of them include the Read Aloud feature. With it, you can have your emails, and messages read to you. The Translator for Outlook feature also helps translate your messages to any language you want. Note that this feature must first be enabled with the Translate feature within the home panel.

Outlook works for several types of email accounts. Below are some more detailed classifications;

1. Outlook can be used to launch any email account from your Internet carrier.

2. Outlook can launch email accounts based on the web. An example of such is the Outlook.com program, owned by Microsoft.
3. Outlook can launch Microsoft Exchange Mail accounts if an exchange server hosts it on a joint network.

When using Outlook, you only need one email account to access all of the features and tools incorporated into it. However, you can have more than one email account running on Outlook. With that out of the way, did you know that you need to get your Outlook configured before thoroughly enjoying all it offers? How can that be done?

The first email account you create on this application is usually linked tightly to the details you present. First, the configuration of your Outlook account means you create a profile and enter all the details for your account. You would also have to give the location of your files and the location of your emails. The procedures below are more detailed descriptions of the configuration process.

1. Launch the Outlook app.
2. If it's your first time running the app, you'd see a page with the title; Sign In to Set Up Office.
3. From the page above, you can either sign into an already existing account or create a new account. Note that the new email account would be an Outlook.com email account.
4. If you need to set up the Outlook app, click the Sign In tab. You'd be directed to the 'Activate Office' display. It is there you'd type in your email address and then click the Next icon.
5. You'd be prompted to present the password to your email account. Type that in and then click the Next icon.

6. The email you presented will then be set within the details of your Outlook account. Once that is done, you'd find receiving and sending emails easy.

After doing the first email link-up, you may need to link up more email accounts. How can you get that done? Check the steps below;

1. Click the File tab.
2. Click the Info option.
3. Click the Add Account option.
4. You would then be redirected to the window for the Outlook app. There, Outlook would search through your device for any other email address.
5. On the window, you'd see a bar for the email address you want to add.
6. Click the Connect tab.
7. You'd be asked to present the password to the email account.

If you have issues configuring the account by Outlook, you'd have to type in the account details manually. First, ensure that you have the correct email address entered. After that, click the link for Advanced Options. Click the Let Me Set Up my Account manually. Note that you'd be clicking a checkbox. Click Connect to continue with your manual setup. You would then be directed to a dialog box for the feature where you'd be prompted to choose the specific type of account you want to add to your Outlook account. The types of accounts include the following;

1. **Microsoft 365:** This is the account that the subscribers of the Office 365 suite have access to. With this account, you are assured of an email environment very similar to the one provided by the Exchange Server software.
2. **Outlook.com:** This account is hosted by the Microsoft team. If you have this account, it means you also have a free Microsoft ID and email. The functions of

an outlook account are very similar to an IMAP account. It also can stand in as an Active Sync Exchange tool for some services on Microsoft.

3. **Exchange:** This account is also hosted by Microsoft. The Microsoft team sourced all the features you'd find on it.

4. **Google:** We all have Google accounts, and the Gmail app is what you're most familiar with. It can be configured as a POP or IMAP account. It also allows you access to the other services made available by Google.

5. **POP:** This term stands for Post Office Protocol. It is another of the very effective ways by which you can send and receive mail.

6. **IMAP:** This term stands for Internet Message Access Protocol. With this tool, you can view all your emails from a server. When your emails are placed on a server, you can access them whenever, irrespective of your device.

7. **Exchange 2013 or earlier:** Outlook has covered you if your email account is the old version of the Exchange app. Click this option if you worked with the early Exchange apps.

If you need to create a new profile on Outlook, follow the steps below. But before then, note that new profiles are the platforms through which you can work on your old Outlook profiles.

1. Click the dialog box for the Mail Setup option.

2. Click the Show Profiles option.

3. The Mail dialog box would then be displayed with the highlight on the General tab.

4. Click Add.

5. A new dialog box for the New Profile feature would then show up.

6. Enter the new name for the new profile.

7. Click the OK tab.

Let's also see how you can create personal file folders on Outlook. These personal file folders are great if you are working on a new project and need a separate file for the emails pertaining to that project. Check the procedures below to get started;

1. Click the Home tab.

2. Click the New Items feature within the 'New' group.

3. Click More Items.

4. Click Outlook Data file.

5. The Create or Open Outlook data file dialog box would then pop up.

6. The dialog box bears details about your file types.

7. Enter a name for the new data file and then click the OK tab.

Setting up your Email Account

Setting Up Your Account

Since there are several ways to set up an account in Outlook, we will use the most common example for those with personal emails that have accounts on platforms such as Gmail, Yahoo, or Hotmail. If you open the program for the first time, you will see a welcome screen with instructions. If this is not the first time, you will have to manually look for the place to do this.

First, go to the actual file tab in the ribbon and select account settings. A dialogue box will open, and it is in the first tab, email, that you should go to. There, you will click on the button new that has a small envelope to add your account. Another box will open, and you should enter your address there. Next, select the button connect and fill in the relevant information that the system requests: name, email address, and password. After you are done, click the button next. You might be actually asked to enter your password again. If not, click on finish, and your account will be set up.

Once you are done, you will be taken to your inbox where you will receive all of your messages and be able to manage them. The home tab of the ribbon will give you access to most of the features regarding messages. In fact, the ribbon for Outlook is relatively simple and has only four tabs apart from the help and file ones.

Setting a Signature

One of the main things a user will want to do when using Outlook is create a signature. To create one, open a new message. You won't necessarily be typing one, but it will give you access to setting the signature that you want to use. Once the message is open, you will see the option signature under the include section of the message tab of the ribbon. Click on the button and select signatures. A new dialogue box should open where you will add the information that you want.

Click on new to start a new signature and establish a name for it. This is the name that will appear in the drop-down menu for you to add signatures if you choose not to do so automatically. Inside the bottom box, the largest of all, where it says edit signature, you will type in what you want to have as the signoff for your messages. Here, you can format font, color, and other style information that is common to other Suite applications.

Once you are done, you can choose in what circumstances this signature will appear. This choice will be established in the right-hand menu, choose default signature, where you can choose from one or more signatures (in case you have more than one). Here you will assign a signature for what email account you wish to add, what signature you want to use for new messages, and what ones will be used for replies and forwards.

Although you have set a signature, you can choose to leave these previous fields blank and only insert the signature in the messages you select. To do this, you will set the signature and click on ok without setting these features up. Every time that you prepare to send a message, you can go back to the signature button and select which one you want to use for that specific message.

Organizing your Inbox

When learning how to organize emails in Outlook, understanding how to use folders and categories is vital. These arc the key tools that you will use in your effort to gain a better handle on the contents of your inbox.

Folders

Folders in Outlook are accessed by clicking the arrow to the left of your inbox, which is located beneath your email address (this is also called the Navigation Pane). There are two types of folders, which are as follows:

- **Default Folders:** The default folders that come with your Microsoft Outlook application are the typical folders that are used in email. You should be familiar with these folders. The most typical ones are draughts, sent mail, deleted items, trash, spam, and other default folders. Other default folders include trash and spam.

- **Personal Folders:** Make sure all of your incoming correspondence is well-organized and prioritized by creating additional folders. It is essential to avoid creating an excessive number of folders since doing so might lead you to get confused about which folder to choose.

How Folders Operate

The user interface for the mail portion of Outlook is composed of a few different components. These tools are designed to assist you in organizing your emails in some way. These components ensure that your mail is organized and sorted properly. Listed below are some of them:

Inbox

The inbox is the location that is largely responsible for storing any new mail that has been received. The instant you launch Outlook, it will immediately begin loading in the background. In addition to the functions of the inbox, it also displays invites for meetings and alerts you if there is a response to one of your messages. The viewing and reading parts make up the outlook interface, respectively. The contents of the inbox are shown in the watching area, while those that are chosen in the viewing section are displayed in the reading section.

Sent Items

The folder referred to as Items That Have Been Sent in Outlook stores copies of items that you have previously sent using Outlook. The primary purpose of it is to store the stuff that you have sent.

Drafts

It is a folder that stores copies of emails that you are drafting but have not yet sent. Additionally, it saves copies of the messages that you have not yet sent, which is useful when you don't want to send them right away but do want to send them at a later time. After returning to the folder, you will be able to access the draught and continue producing the document.

The Deleted Items folder

Items from other folders that you have removed from Outlook and moved to this folder are preserved here.

Junk Emails

Outlook classifies an email as junk mail if it were sent to you by someone the program does not recognize or that you do not feel comfortable trusting.

Archive

The Archive folder in Outlook stores preserved messages that you may choose to hide from other users. Your most critical emails will be stored securely in this folder.

Notes

The Notes function may be used to jot down personal information and to keep track of ongoing tasks. Using the Notes feature of Outlook, you may save vital information that you do not want to lose and that you do not want to be forgotten. From this location, you'll be able to see the notes that you've generated. You can go to your Notes by choosing "Note" in the bar that runs across the top of the screen.

Categories

The use of categories makes it easy to color code your communications. It is actually and entirely up to you whether or not you, for instance, designate the color red to indicate communications that demand urgent attention, the color green to indicate messages that require prompt action, the color purple to indicate meetings, and so on. There are a variety of applications for using color coding. You will want to devise a plan that is tailored to your specific needs. When your inbox is organized using color-coded categories, it is much simpler to have an option that lets you go through your messages and decide what to do with each one with just a quick look.

Creating and Sending Emails

You have already seen how to start a new message in order to create a signature. This feature is available by clicking on the new email button. The message box will appear, and you will type in your message. You will be able to format it as you wish by using the text format tools in the ribbon; however, be aware that not necessarily all receivers will be able to see the formatting. This will depend on the program that they have and their viewing functionalities.

While the message's to and the cc (carbon copy) are readily available, the bcc (blind carbon copy) is not, and you will need to manually add it. To do so, click on the to or the cc buttons for a dialogue box with the option of bcc to appear. Type in one address and press ok to continue. Another way to expose the bcc field is to go to the options tab in the ribbon and under the show fields section, you will see the options bcc and from. Click on each of these buttons to see the referred field and change any information you wish regarding what you can see.

It is also in the options tab that you will be able to request that the receiver sends a receipt that they have received or that they have read the message. Click on each of these boxes to select what will happen to the messages you send. You can choose to apply these to all your messages, in which case you will receive a notification every time an actual message is read and received.

Delayed Delivery

Sometimes when you send a message, you do not want it to be delivered immediately, opting for it to be delivered the next morning, for example. This can actually be done by setting up the message's configuration as well. In the options tab, you will have a more options section that will allow you to use the delay delivery option. Once you click on this option, a dialogue box will open for you to type in the relevant information. You can determine when you want the message to be delivered, to whom you want the answers to be sent to, and after how much time the message should expire.

Determining Importance

One of the features that comes along with having Outlook is being able to apply a high or a low priority to your message. This can actually be done by clicking on the exclamation mark for establishing a high priority or on the blue arrow pointing down for emails with low priority.

You can also determine if the message will need any follow up by clicking on the red flag. When you do, a drop-down menu will expand, and you can choose when you want the program to give you a reminder to follow it up. Although the program allows you to choose from some standard options, you can also set up your own reminder by customizing the date.

Polling Through Email

Sometimes we send emails to groups of people because we want their approval on something. Did you actually know that you can use a polling tool that is within Outlook so that the answers get back to you? This can also be defined when you are writing the message in the options tab.

In the tracking options, there will be a button named use voting buttons. By clicking on it, a drop-down menu will become available where the receivers of the message can choose from accept or reject or yes, no, and maybe. If you want to, you can also personalize these buttons in the dialogue box by separating the options by a semicolon.

Adding Attachments and Images

Did you know that you can add pictures and images to the body of the message without it being an attachment? However, once again, it is important to be aware that not all people might receive it in the message but rather as an attachment. This will depend on their configuration. Use the features on the ribbon to add accordingly—they will work similarly to what we have seen in the previous chapters.

However, adding an attachment will depend on the size that your service provider allows. Gmail, for example, only allows attachments of up to 5GB. If the file, or files, is within the allowed value, then you can add them to the message by clicking on the attach file button that is available both in the home and insert tabs of the ribbon. Once you click on the button, it will open a list of recent files that you have opened or allow you to browse your computer to look for others.

There are also two other ways to attach files to your message. The first is to actually drag and drop the file or files in the message window. Doing this will automatically place the file within the message that you will send. The other way to add files is to copy and paste them into the message window. Both ways of attaching files are valid and will allow you to send them to the receiver.

Pro tip: To remove the files you have attached, just click on them and press delete on your keyboard. This will automatically delete them and need to be attached again if you decide to place them back.

Out-of-Office Messages

One of the most useful things to actually have in your email is an automatic reply that others will receive if you are temporarily unavailable to read your messages. Also known as actually an out of office message, these will be configured so that each time that you go on vacation, for example, people will be warned that you cannot be reached, that you do not have access to your messages, or any other message that you wish to convey.

To apply the message, you need to go to the file tab and select automatic replies (out of office) that will be available under account information. Once you are there, you will see the option to send automatic replies. Check this box. If the message is a general one that users will receive when they contact you, then establishing a date is not necessary. However, if you want to establish a date for when senders will get this message, click on the only send during this time range option.

In the box that comes after, you will be able to write the message and add your signature. Even though these messages will be received by those who send you messages, you will still continue to access your messages normally. Once you are done writing what you want to communicate, click ok and the feature is already set.

Pro tip: If you want to deactivate the out of office messages, you can do so by clicking on the yellow banner that will appear on your Outlook page when you open it. It will have a button written turn off that you will be able to click, or you can actually go to the file tab and click on turn off in the automatic replies section.

Managing Your Calendar

Managing your time and schedule on Outlook involves you knowing when to create your meetings and cancel any meeting you won't be available for. For the creation of sessions, you'd need to provide the time and date for the discussion. You'd also need to give the theme and location of the meeting. The last thing you'd need to do is invite your contacts to the forum. The invitation process is usually done from the Contacts folder. You'd click the contacts you want to send the meeting invitation to. If you have several invitations to send, you could create a group and then add the contacts to it. That way, things become easy over time.

Click the Meeting feature within the Communicate group. A dialog box for the Meeting would immediately pop up. You'd also see the selected contacts in the 'To box.' Click the Address Book tool within the Attendees group to add more contacts. You'd be required to type out a theme for the meeting in the Subject box. The Location box is where you type out where the meeting will go. For example, it could be a conference room, an organization, etc. You'd also need to type out the time the meeting would start and when it would end.

Teams

Microsoft Teams is a powerful tool that takes the process of interacting and talking with other members of your team to a whole new level. Using Microsoft Teams, it is possible to collaborate from any location, regardless of the number of people doing so—two, three, or even ten thousand. The notion of working remotely is gaining popularity among teams located all over the globe. Microsoft's goal is to maintain connectivity amongst teams even when members are located in various physical places. To this end, Microsoft Teams is being made accessible to as many people as possible. There is no need to go somewhere else since teams allow you to have conversations, meetings, phone calls, study sessions, and cooperate all in the same place. Continue reading for some useful advice on working from home, and don't forget to sign up for Teams so you can start using it for free right now. The 'future of workplaces' is brought to life by

Microsoft Teams, which lives up to its name. Teams are designed to facilitate collaborative work amongst co-workers via the exchange of files, participation in chats, and even participation in voice and video conversations. Microsoft Teams is designed to accommodate the ever-evolving needs of today's contemporary workplace, in contrast to the document libraries and task lists that are part of SharePoint, which represent more or less permanent data repositories. It's possible that during the course of a year, you'll find yourself playing for many different teams. You may find yourself engaging in many channels while being part of the same team. This book explains the concepts of teams and channels. It demonstrates how to inform colleagues when you are busy or available for collaborations, how to start a discussion with them, as well as how to have a private talk with them. You may get up and running more quickly by using Microsoft Teams for your video conferencing and communication needs. This will assist ensure that your needs are met. Examine the specifics of this component to have an understanding of how it may most effectively serve your team.

Introduction to Microsoft Teams

What is Microsoft Teams?

Microsoft Teams is a software application that facilitates communication and collaboration between users working on shared projects. It provides a central location for users to exchange messages, files, and other information related to the project. Microsoft Teams allows users to easily share files and ideas, work on tasks together, and stay up-to-date on the latest project developments. This makes collaboration and communication much simpler and more efficient. Microsoft Teams can help you stay connected and get the job done, whether working on a small team project or a significant corporate initiative. Teams consolidates communications, chat history, files, and applications into a single platform, enabling users to stay organized and efficiently collaborate with others. As long as users feel confident that their data is secure, they can use any device they want. Teams is an application designed to help users work together more effectively by providing chat-based communication and collaboration tools. Teams provides a platform for users to stay organized and connected with their teammates, which can help improve workflows and productivity.

Microsoft Teams uses Azure Active Directory to store and manage user identity information. This makes it simpler for employers to sign in and enter the necessary information, thereby improving the user experience. Azure AD makes it easier to manage user identities and permissions within Teams and create and manage teams within Azure AD. This allows teams to collaborate effectively and work together efficiently. Creating a team in Teams automatically generates a SharePoint Online site and an Exchange Online group mailbox. This gives your team a shared space to store files and work together and a shared inbox for communications. This provides your team with storage space for files and a platform for communication. This allows teams to connect easily with other Office 365 services, which enhances productivity and collaboration. The Teams chat service provides users with capabilities such as archiving and eDiscovery, similar to those in Office 365. This is an excellent option for businesses using a chat service that integrates with their existing Office 365 tools. This tool is valuable for companies and organizations because it allows them to keep track of their communications and helps to improve communication efficiency. This enables users to utilize these capabilities for the data being exchanged in Teams.

Setting up a Team

To get down to the actual nitty-gritty of the situation, all of these things have to be put into practice to enjoy all of the advantages that have previously been mentioned. When using Microsoft Teams, a "Team" refers to a group of people that collaborate toward the achievement of a certain objective; in many cases, the whole of a company will be included in a single Team. In the meanwhile, Channels function similarly to subgroups that are a part of the organization. They are divided into groups, with each group being committed to a certain department, project, or piece of work. Imagine, for the sake of this illustration, that Teams is a corporation and Channels is the sales division of that same organization. Therefore, channels are made after a team has already been established.

The following procedures may be followed to set up channels and teams:

Create a Team

Launch the Microsoft Teams program, and from the choices accessible at the bottom of the Teams sidebar on the left, pick "Join or create a team." In the new screen that has just been shown, click the button labeled "Create a team." On the screen that follows, you will be given a choice between selecting:

- Establish a brand-new team from the ground up; this will be a fresh group of players.
- Make a new team by cloning an existing group or team in Office 365.

If your team was previously using Office 365 before migrating to Teams, you might already have groups that can be imported by utilizing the option to "Create from..." If your team was already using Office 365 before moving to Teams, you might already have groups that can be imported. If this is not the case, you may go through with the plan to "Build a team from scratch." After that, you should choose the individuals that will make up the team. Consider the following factors while making your decision, keeping in mind how you want the structure and organization of your platform to look:

Private

Choose this option for situations in which a group needs to consist of no more than a select few individuals, as an example.

Public

The public is the optimal setting for groups that are constantly reorganizing their membership rosters.

The Org-Wide

The Org-Wide option is the one you should go with if you want to host your whole organization on the platform as a single 'team' and use channels to divide up the work and ensure that everyone is on the same page when it comes to communication.

- After settling on the composition of the group that you want to put together, the next step is to give it a name.
- After providing an appropriate team name, such as 'Sales' or 'Social Media,' click the 'Create' button located in the very bottom right corner of the screen to finish creating the team.
- After you have finished creating your new team, your new team will immediately appear on the new page.
- You may add members to the team by either clicking on the three dots that are located next to the Team name from anywhere in the team app or by using the 'Add additional people' option that is located on the homepage of the Teams app. Simply type in the names of the people whose participation you want to be required for the group.
- You might offer them guest access instead, using their email address as both a login and a password, if they are considered to be "guests," which refers to individuals who are not affiliated with your organization.

Make a Channel

After a team has been created, it is time to start including channels in the group that has been created. In order to collaborate effectively as a team, you need to have channels. When Microsoft Teams is initially started up, it will immediately create a general channel that will be accessible to all members of the team. It is possible to add more channels. To begin, go to the team you would want to add a new channel to and click the menu option that reads "Create additional channel." On the homepage of the Team website is a link that reads "Create more channels." You will be able to choose a name for the channel from the menu that appears, provide a description for the channel, and change the privacy settings so that either all team members or only a select few team members can view the information. All of these options will actually be available in the pop-up window that appears. After you have done customizing the channel, you can begin the process of creating it by clicking the 'Add' button in the configuration window.

Defining Your Status

When you indicate your status, it is much simpler for your co-workers to determine whether or not they may communicate with you. Make it a practice to update your status so that other members of the team always know whether or not they can contact you and how to do so. In order to manage your status inside Teams, follow these steps:

- Open your user menu. The menu may be accessed by looking in the top-right-hand corner of the screen. When you open it, a drop-down menu appears before you.
- When the status option, which is the first choice on the menu, is selected, a drop-down menu with other status choices will appear.
- Pick one of the options: Available, Busy, or another one.

Consider the scenario in which you need to determine if a co-worker is free, occupied, or absent. Start entering the name of your co-worker in the Search box actually located at the very top of the screen once you have moved your mouse there. Your colleague's name needs to be included on a list that may be dropped down. Simply click on the name of the person you are conversing with to get to that person's page.

Chatting and Collaborating with Team Members

Conversations aren't a mystery if you're familiar with social media platforms like Facebook or LinkedIn. You can contribute to a discussion by posting, commenting on the postings made by others, and liking a post. Conversations amongst employees are about more than just talking about a certain subject. Dialogue may also serve as an essential record of a subject, its history, or its context. Newcomers to a channel are able to catch up on the latest developments in a project by simply browsing the dialogue that is taking place in that channel. Co-workers can evaluate a discussion to determine how far along a project is, discover what questions have been asked in the past, and investigate the history of a project to see how it has developed over time. On these pages, you'll find instructions on how to save a discussion as a bookmark, add a conversation to your favorites, start new conversations, and respond to existing ones.

Liking and Bookmarking Conversations

To like a discussion and add it to your bookmarks in Teams, follow these steps:

- Proceed to a channel's Conversations page when you're ready.
- When you enter a channel, the Conversations page is the first page that you see.
- Move your actual mouse pointer over one of the posts.

You will see the following three buttons:

More options

Opens a drop-down list with choices for flagging a post as unopened, copying a hyperlink to the post to the Clipboard, or accessing the post in Immersive Reader. Clicking the More Options button opens the drop-down list. Within Microsoft Teams, there is a unique view called Immersive Reader that makes it simpler to read through lengthy chats.

Save the message

This function will save the message so that you may examine it at a later time. To access posts that have been saved, visit the user menu and choose Saved from the list of options.

Like the message

This user likes the post. Everyone on the team may see the posts that you liked.

You have numerous options at your disposal when interacting with channel postings, including the ability to like them and save them for later use.

Beginning a Conversation

To get a discussion started, just follow these steps:

- Proceed to a channel's Conversations page when you're ready.
- Please provide your message in the space provided.
- Tools for inputting emojis, hyperlinks, and other goodies are located underneath the text field in the document. In order to inform a colleague about the discussion, you want to begin, write the at symbol (@) followed by the colleague's name into the text box. This will alert the colleague about the conversation you intend to begin.

You can attach the discussion to other channels in addition to alerting the other participants. Followed by the at symbol (@), type the name of the channel you want to join. You may send the message by pressing Enter or the Send button. Every member of the team can hear and see what you are saying.

Responding to a Conversation

To publish a response in response to a chat, follow these steps:

- Proceed to a channel's Conversations page when you're ready.
- Click the Reply button that is located in the message to which you wish to respond.
- After you have finished typing your message, either hit the Enter key or select the Send button.

Having a Confidential Conversation with a Colleague

There are instances in which some individuals in a team should not voice their inquiries, criticisms, or worries. There are instances when the content of a communication is best kept between two persons or a small group of carefully chosen employees. Make sure your interactions stay under wraps by using the Chat function. When using Teams, you should never make a remark that you wouldn't want your manager or IT administrator to see. Even a chat message that is only supposed to be intended for a small group of people cannot be considered really private. Administrators of Teams can audit and access all material included inside a Teams workspace. This is done for purposes of both security and regulatory compliance. Follow these instructions to begin a private conversation with one or two individuals of your choice and to take part in the conversation:

- To start a new conversation, choose the New Chat button located on the navigation bar that runs along the top of the screen.
- You may access the New Chat option by looking to the left of the Search box for the symbol that resembles a pen and paper.
- A list of recent users will show whenever you start a new conversation or participate in an existing one on the Chat page. If you wish to take up where you left off with a prior chat, you may choose a name to do so.
- After entering your message, make sure you hit Enter.

- You are presented with a Chat window.

When someone wishes to talk with you, a notice will appear in the bottom-right corner of the screen. Simply clicking on this notice will bring up the Chat window, where you can then begin conversing. To send a message, type it into the box labeled "Type a New Message," then either press Enter or click the Send button To bring in other participants to a conversation, choose the "Add People" option. The location of this button may be found in the top-right-hand corner of the display.

Sharing Files and Resources

It's possible that you'll need to add other applications like Planner, To-Do, and Sway to make use of them inside the Microsoft Teams app; however, this is a simple process as long as the app in question is included in your subscription. Launch Teams, then use the search bar at the bottom left to find and add your preferred application; keep in mind that it must be compatible with your membership. The screen that displays the app's description will appear after you have selected the app that you desire. Spend a little time going over all of the different subsections (e.g., Tabs, Messages, Personal app.) This section will outline the capabilities of the application, as well as how and where it will be accessible inside Teams, allowing you to utilize it as is or modify it as you see fit. After that, choose the Add button, and at that point, your app will be accessible for use inside the app that your team uses.

Linking up Streams with Teams

Microsoft Stream is a corporate video solution that provides you with the capacity to develop and securely distribute videos inside your own organization. Stream is easy to use in many aspects. You and your other employees can work together on videos by utilizing applications that you are already acquainted with, like SharePoint, Teams, and Yammer, in addition to a web browser. Microsoft Stream incorporates enterprise search, complete with smart search capabilities and intelligent searching, as a standard feature. Because of this, it is easy to generate and distribute content, as well as to obtain the information you want at the time you require it. Microsoft Stream is the replacement for Office 365 Video, and your Office 365 Video accounts will be converted to Microsoft Stream. If you have previously used Office 365 Video, you should be aware that Microsoft Stream is the successor to Office 365 Video. If you are actually worried about the safety of uploading your videos to a service that is located outside of your firewall but would still want some assistance, Microsoft Stream can provide it. Enterprise-level protection is provided for Microsoft Stream, just as it is for the other components of the Office 365 suite. Because your users have signed in, they have access to videos, and the permission levels on particular films may be modified to restrict access to some users while allowing others to view. When utilizing Microsoft Stream, you can choose who you want to share content with, whether it be a select group of individuals on your team or the whole of your company. Using Microsoft Stream, everybody in your company can take part in and benefit from video collaboration, and the platform ensures that every video is kept secure. Microsoft Stream also helps organize video material into channels and categories, making it simpler to find what you're looking for when you need it.

Organize Using Channels and Groups

Channels are an excellent tool for classifying and organizing the available content. You may bookmark videos or rapidly follow a channel to make sure you don't miss any new ones that are uploaded. If you are a subscriber, this part of the homepage will enable you to see any new videos that have been uploaded to a channel and will make it simple to locate the channel that you follow. Click the Following button to stop following a channel that you are no longer interested in. However, Stream's Groups are modeled around Office 365 Groups in both appearance and functionality. When you create a group in Stream, it will automatically build a new Office 365 Group. This group will have its own email address, calendar, and site that can be accessed throughout Office 365. If your company already makes use of Office 365 Groups in other places, such as Microsoft Teams, SharePoint, Yammer, or Planner, you can immediately begin utilizing them in Stream. While channels are primarily used for organizing videos into sections and authors, groups are developed specifically to impose restrictions on video permissions. To a greater extent, groups take measures to limit the audience for their videos.

The Option of Creating Live Events

It is usually recommended by Microsoft that you configure your video, community, and user rights at least twenty-four hours before the event to have the best possible experience. This may be shown by, among other things, the addition of users, the modification of video permissions, or the transition of a community from private to public status. It may actually take up to two hours for some changes to take effect in Microsoft Stream, Microsoft Teams, and Microsoft Yammer. Testing may be done, and adjustments can be made, if required, after at least twenty-four hours have passed.

Hosting Virtual Meetings

Meetings may be held in one of two ways using Teams. You and a colleague have the option of participating in a meeting via the use of audio or video technology, or you can go back to the tried-and-true method of setting up a face-to-face appointment on a certain day and hour.

Holding a Conference (Audio or Video)

To successfully host a video or audio meeting, proceed with the following steps:

- Find the person you are hoping to speak with.
- Carry out a global search or look for the person's user symbol in the chat history or Chat window on your device.
- When you open a person's user card, you may access it by clicking on the person's name.
- A person's name and a picture of that individual are both printed on the card.

- Click the button labeled "Video Call" or "Audio Call" located on the user card.
- The recipient of your call will be notified that you have placed a call to them. At this point, the individual has the option of either declining or accepting the call.
- Simply pressing a button on the user card will get the call started.

You may conduct the chat or end it by using the buttons that are located at the bottom of the Call window:

Webcam: Switches the webcam on/off

Microphone: Controls microphone's muting/unmuting

Sharing: Let other participants view your screen

More Options: Provides an additional menu for putting the call on hold, transferring, and other options

Hang Up: Terminates the ongoing call

Setting up a Meeting and Sending out Invitations to Participants

To arrange a face-to-face meeting with a fellow worker, please proceed as follows:

- In the navigation bar, choose the Meetings tab to get started.
- Simply click the Meeting Scheduling button.
- Using the New Meeting box, provide a summary of the gathering and ask others to join you there.
- Give the gathering a title, decide where it will take place, specify when it will take place, and invite the appropriate employees.
- To see your schedule, click the icon.

- Your calendar has been updated to reflect the meeting.
- Colleagues are notified in the form of a message that a meeting is being requested. Invitees may respond to the communication by clicking one of three buttons—Accept, Tentative, or Decline—that are included in the message. When a meeting request is approved, it is added to the calendar straight away.

OneDrive

Introduction to Microsoft OneDrive

Probably one of the fastest growing sectors in recent years is the cloud, whether cloud computing, cloud gaming, or simple cloud for data storage, a function for which it was born a few years ago. Users' aversion to putting their data on the network and not on their own device is gradually diminishing, and more and more people are turning to the cloud because of its immediacy and the convenience of having data always available on as many devices as possible. In addition, prices have definitely come down compared to the past, with many cloud services providing some space for free, which has increased users exponentially. Among the many cloud services available, one of the most used, integrated and popular is definitely Microsoft OneDrive, which has the great advantage of having the entire Microsoft infrastructure behind it, thus with integration with the Office package and, above all, with Windows.

What is Microsoft OneDrive?

You are probably familiar with Microsoft OneDrive, especially if you have a Windows device, since it is already preinstalled and running even without the user actually using it. Basically OneDrive is a personal cloud storage space, analogous to services such as iCloud, Google Drive or Dropbox to name a few of the most popular. For those who do not know what a cloud storage space is, the explanation is very simple: it is like having a storage device, imagine a hard drive or a USB stick, but it is not physical and you do not have to plug it into your PC to see the data, since it is stored in server rooms scattered around the world. So the data is not physically in our PC or on a device that we can touch, but it is ideally on the cloud, hence the term cloud.

The cloud has great advantages over storing on a physical device in our PC, in the first instance the security of not losing the data accidentally, in fact a hard disk can break, a USB stick can be lost, while the data on the cloud is not lost, it remains saved without the possibility of losing it. The second major advantage of the cloud is the accessibility of data, if you have documents on your hard disk on your PC, those documents will be accessible only and exclusively if you have your PC with you, while the data on the cloud can be accessed from anywhere on the globe and with any device, you only need to log in with your own credentials, no small convenience. Of course, the cloud brings with it one disadvantage that still drives many people away from using it, and that is data security. In the history of the cloud, there are very famous and blatant breaches that have led to the disclosure of personal data and documents, especially of famous people. There is no full assurance that these things will never happen again, but it is true that security over the years has increased exponentially, partly because of these attacks.

Microsoft OneDrive is available in two plans, one dedicated to individuals, and one dedicated to businesses. Let's look specifically at the two plans.

Personal

The personal plan, which is also for the family, starts with a free basic plan with 5 GB of OneDrive space, which can be expanded up to 100 GB with 2 euros per month. Then we get to the more substantial plans, with the Microsoft 365 Personal plan, designed for one person, which includes 1 TB of OneDrive storage and the availability of the entire basic Office package. If you want OneDrive for the whole family there is the Family plan that includes 1 TB of OneDrive space for each person with up to 6 people and the basic Office package.

Business

For the business side, you obviously do not start with a free plan, but with a basic plan that includes 1 TB of space for each user, which then expands with Plan 2 that expands both security and available space. Then we come to the richer plans, such as Basic which includes 1 TB per user and the use of certain services such as Teams or Exchange. The richest plan Business Standard which includes virtually the entire Microsoft ecosystem, with the full Office package and also all other applications such as Teams or Yammer.

Main Strengths

OneDrive's main strengths are synchronization and cross-platform compatibility. OneDrive, in fact, allows you to create files on your PC and edit it on your tablet or smartphone, saving all the changes you make. It is compatible with Windows Phone, Android, iOS and even Xbox.

As a result, you may access the same content from any device, rather than needing to email it or store it to a memory stick. OneDrive lets you see real-time changes and retrieve all prior versions of the same document. Changes may also be made by another person with access to the file, enabling you to work on the same project with ease while avoiding the propagation of several copies of the same. OneNote, Excel, PowerPoint, and Word files may all be created and edited in the cloud using OneDrive.

With Microsoft OneDrive, you can safely access your files from anywhere. All you need is a gadget and an Internet connection. After syncing the cloud folder on your desktop, you may even view them without a connection.

Another advantage that should not be overlooked is security. Your data are always safe on OneDrive. All changes you make are immediately stored on all synced devices, so you don't have to worry about backing up every time. All you have to actually do is enable the auto-save feature to avoid data loss.

Setting up your OneDrive Account

Do you have an email account with Microsoft? - Outlook or Microsoft Live. Consider yourself to be the owner of a OneDrive account if you have any of these capabilities. Easy, isn't it? Launch your web browser, sign in to Office 365 using the email address you use for the service, and then pick OneDrive from the menu on the sidebar to get access to the cloud storage service. This will allow you to access your OneDrive account. After that, you will be sent to a user interface that shows all of the documents that you have saved in other Office 365 applications like Word, Excel, PowerPoint, and others. You also can upload a new file of any kind, which may be done at any time. OneDrive now works better for those who already have a Microsoft account, thanks to improvements made by Microsoft. When you actually sign up for a Microsoft account, a storage space in OneDrive is immediately added to your account. One unknown thing is whether or if Microsoft is using this method as part of a commercial effort to attract more customers to their cloud storage. Even while the introduction of OneDrive was a welcome development for the cloud storage system, the vast majority of users are having trouble mastering its interface. When it comes to online storage, the fact that OneDrive performs the same functions as Google Drive and other cloud storage programs is a fascinating development to notice. This is because OneDrive provides you with an entirely web-based location for putting or storing your files. To access your data or files, you will first need to sign in to your Microsoft account. This is similar to the process required by other cloud storage applications.

Sign up with OneDrive

When you join up with Microsoft OneDrive, there are several steps you must do, including the following:

- To access OneDrive, go to OneDrive.live.com. You will then be actually presented with the screen shown below, where you will pick "sign up for free."
- Pick the kind of account you want to use. In this scenario, you will have to choose between establishing a personal account and a company account in order to proceed. If you have a business account, the services that are available to you are not free; rather, you must pay a fee to use them.
- Simply enter your email address below. There is a spot for you to input your email address, and if you don't already have one, you have the option to make one for yourself.
- Please enter a new password. After entering your password, you will be prompted to click the "next" button.

Other details at this point, you are asked to provide both your birth date and the country in which you were born. Your email address is awaiting verification. When all of these steps have been completed, a confirmation code will be issued to your phone number or email address so that we can verify that you are actually the rightful owner of the email or phone number. After that, you will be asked to put in the code so that it may be validated. Confirmation in its final form and the establishment of an account In this section, you will need to demonstrate that you are a human by entering the captcha code accurately. Once you have done so, your account will be established, and you will then be able to upload your files and documents to your account.

Sign in to your OneDrive Account

You may sign in to OneDrive in one of two ways: either via the web page or through the application. If you already have the specific app installed on your device, then you may sign in by following the steps outlined in the section below. In contrast, if the application is not already installed on your computer, you will need to either download it to use it or log in to your account through the website (OneDrive.live.com).

- You will begin by going to the Start menu and typing "OneDrive" into the search bar that appears.
- When the search is complete, you will notice OneDrive among the results; to access it, click on its name. If you already have a OneDrive account, all you need to do is enter the email address that you used to register for the account and then click the "sign in" button.
- After that, go to the next page and input your password there. You will be asked to input an extra code that has been given to either your email address or phone number for correct confirmation of account ownership. This code will be supplied to you if you have already set up some other method of authentication for your Microsoft account.
- To pick the OneDrive folder you desire, you must first follow the guidelines that are provided. If you have previously logged in to this computer, there is a chance that the OneDrive folder was already present on your computer. You have the option of clicking here to utilize this folder or selecting the option to pick a new folder.

Uploading and Organizing Files

After creating the account and logging in, you will be looking at your personal OneDrive space, accessible only to you with your credentials, from any device you want. Below we are going to look at how to manage our files and folders on OneDrive, it is a very simple process, similar to what we normally do with files physically on our PC.

Create Files and Folders

The first thing we need to do to put documents inside OneDrive is to understand how to create folders to organize them, but also how to create files directly from OneDrive. The procedure is very simple, once you log into the OneDrive web application you will be faced with your empty cloud space, or with a few preset folders. To create new files and folders you will have to click on the New button in the top bar. A drop-down menu will open for you where you can decide what to create, if you want to create a folder click on the relevant item, otherwise you can directly create documents through the whole Office package or plain text documents, as if it were a notepad on the web.

Uploading the Files and Folders from your PC

Uploading files and folders that already exist on our PC to put them on the cloud and have them available everywhere is a very simple and straightforward procedure, just like that of creating a new file or folder. You will need to click on the Upload button in the top bar and decide whether to upload a File or an entire Folder within OneDrive. Click on one of the two choices based on what you want to upload to OneDrive and the window will open for you to browse the files on your PC. You will simply select the desired file or folder and click Open to upload that particular file to OneDrive.

Sort, Filter and View Files

You can sort files on OneDrive on any screen, either on the main screen or within each folder. To sort files you will need to click on the Sort button in the upper right corner. A drop-down menu will open to you with various standard settings such as Name, Last Modified, or File Size, but you can also arrange the screen to your liking with the Rearrange button. A page will open to you where you can move and place files to your liking, eventually you will have to click Save Change to make the change effective.

Open or Download Files

After creating new files or uploading existing files to OneDrive, there is also the need to open them, but also to download them, perhaps from another device where they are not physically present. To open files is very simple, it works like files on Windows, you just search for the file within the folders and click on it to view it. OneDrive allows you to open a lot of files, obviously all Office package files, but also PDFs, images, music files and much more directly from the web application. To download a file you will first have to find it within the resources on OneDrive, you can also use the search bar at the top. Once you find the file or folder you want to download you will have two ways to download it, you can either right-click on it and then select the Download item from the drop-down menu, or select it by clicking on the small white circle that appears in the top right corner when you place your mouse over a file and then click on the Download item that will appear in the top bars. To select multiple files or folders to download at the same time you can use mouse drag and drop while holding down the left mouse button.

Search and Navigate through Files and Folders

Searching through files and folders on OneDrive is very simple. You can either navigate normally as if you were in the Windows Explorer on your Windows PC, or use the search function if you want to find a specific file or folder. Obviously, to search for a specific file or folder you have to remember their name; just type it into the search bar at the top, which is characterized by a magnifying glass and the words Search all items. To better navigate through your OneDrive files you can also use the left-hand menu, where files are divided among various items, such as Recent Items and Photos.

Moving, Copying, and Remaining Files and Folders

Since, as already mentioned, the OneDrive web interface works like a regular Windows folder, to move files you just have to do drag and drop, that is, click and hold the left mouse button on a file or folder and move it where you want it; if you move it over a folder the file will move within that folder. You can also do this by right-clicking over a folder and clicking on the Move To item, a drop-down will open where you can select the destination folder. The procedure for copying a file or folder is the same, except that you will have to click on the Copy to button and select the destination. To rename a file or folder just right-click on it and select Rename.

Deleting or Restoring Files and Folders

To delete a folder or file you will have to right-click on it and select Delete. You can also do this by selecting one or more files and clicking the Delete key on your keyboard. All deleted files, as is the case on Windows, are not deleted altogether, but are moved to the Recycle Bin and thus are easily recoverable. To restore an accidentally deleted file or folder, simply enter the recycle bin from the left-hand menu, select the accidentally deleted file or folder, and click Restore. At this point the file will return to its place as if it had never been deleted.

Sharing Files and Folders with Others

You should make your files available to other people so that they may see, modify, or just view your work. Sharing documents allows many users to work together on a single Office document. From the OneDrive window, you have the option to share either an individual file or a whole folder, which includes all of the files included inside the folder. When you actually share a file with other people, you are effectively giving them permission to either read your file or view it and make changes to it.

Sharing the File Directly

You can share a file directly from Word, Excel, or PowerPoint by clicking the Share button, which can be found in the upper-right-hand corner of the screen. This saves you from actually having to go to the OneDrive window. The Share pane will appear after you have selected OneDrive from the Share window and have then clicked on the Share button. From that location, you may send email invitations to other people to share a file with them or produce a sharing link.

Email Invitation

In order to send the file to other people through email, you must first enter their email addresses into the Invite People text box. After that, choose either Can Edit or Can View from the drop-down menu to see what kind of editing access the sharer has, and then click the Share button. (If you prefer not to input a sharer's email address directly, you may click the Search the Address Book button instead and then use the Address Book dialogue box to choose the person's name.) (If you prefer not to input a sharer's email address directly, you may click the Search the Address Book button instead and then use the Address Book dialogue box to choose the person's name.)

Link Generator

Make the file available to others by creating a link to it: Simply click the Get a Sharing Link button (located at the bottom of the Share pane). Then you may create either an edit link or a view-only link by clicking a button. In the last step, choose the link to copy it to the clipboard by clicking the Copy button. You will then be able to copy the link and eventually paste it into an email or a website.

Email Invitation Process on OneDrive

If you actually want to share a file (or all of the files in a folder), you may do so by following these steps and sending out an email message with links to the files. One simple click is all the person who receives your email message has to do to read or see the file you attached.

- Make your selection in OneDrive of the file or folder you want to share.
- To share content, click the Share icon.
- On the Toolbar that actually runs along the top of the screen in OneDrive, you will notice a button labeled Share.
- You are looking at the Share window
- To determine whether other users are only able to view the file or edit it as well, select or deselect the Allow Editing option.

- Your decision in this section will influence the access rights that are granted to sharers.
- You have the option of imposing a password as well as a time limit on the files that you plan to share with other people.
- Select email account.
- Within the Share window, there are text fields where one may insert their email address and a message
- Simply enter the email addresses of the individuals with whom you want to actually share the folder or file.
- To share content, click the Share icon.

To determine which folders and files are shared, you must first switch the Files window over to List view. When they are shared, the word "Shared" will appear in the Sharing column. You may adjust how files and folders are shared, as well as unshared, at any time by returning to the File window. You can access this window at any time.

Link Generation

To generate a hyperlink that allows you to share a file (or all of the files in a folder), please follow these steps. Once OneDrive has generated the link, you will be able to share it publicly or email it to other people. The file may be seen (or viewed together with editing capabilities) by anybody who hits the link.

- Choose the particular file or folder you wish to share from the menu that appears when you open OneDrive.
- To share content, click the Share icon.
- You may generate a link to a file or folder using the Share window.
- Choose whether you want to allow editing or not.
- Your decision will decide whether other people may access the file as well as change it or whether they can just view it.
- You have the option of putting a password on the files you plan to share as well as setting an expiry date for those files.

- Click the Get a Link button.

This URL was generated by OneDrive, it is shown in the Share window.

Simply choose the button labeled Copy. You are free to post the link anywhere you choose at this point, whether it be on a blog, a website, or an email message.

Sharing a Document or Folder in OneDrive

OneDrive gives you the ability to share your papers while yet giving you full control over those documents. Be aware that your folders and documents will remain private unless you want to share them with others. To make your files accessible to others, follow the steps outlined below:

- Click the tiny circle icon that is located on the file that you want to share to choose it as the file that you want to share. Click the actual "Share" button located in the Toolbar.
- To access further customization choices, go to the popup menu and choose the option that reads, "Anyone who has the link may change."
- Remove the actual checkmark from the box labeled "Allow editing" to prohibit your collaborator from making changes to your work. They will not have access to any other features of your document.
- Whenever you are ready, after you are finished, click the "Apply" button.
- In the "To:" field, enter the email addresses of the recipients, and in the "Message" field, type in a note to alert them about your paper. Simply forward your item by clicking the Send button (s).
- Alternatively, you may manually invite individuals by clicking "Copy link" and sending them the URL that you have copied.

Collaborating on Documents in Real-Time

Accessing Files Shared by Others

To see the names of the folders and files that others have shared with you as well as those that you have shared with others, go to the Shared pane. Clicking the Shared button in the OneDrive navigation pane will take you to the Shared window (located on the left side of the window). You can open files and folders in the Shared Window using the same method that you use to access them in the Files or Recent windows, which is to click on the item. You might also right-click and choose Open from the context-sensitive menu that appears.

Forms

Microsoft Forms is actually a tool that allows users to create surveys, quizzes, and polls easily. It is a part of the Microsoft 365 suite of applications and is accessible through a web browser or as a mobile app.

Using Microsoft Forms, users can create customized surveys and quizzes, and collect responses from participants. The platform offers a variety of question types, including multiple-choice, text, and rating questions, and supports images and videos to make the survey more engaging.

Introduction to Microsoft Forms

Microsoft Forms is an online survey and quiz tool that allows users to create customized forms and quizzes for various purposes, such as feedback collection, event registration, customer satisfaction surveys, employee assessments, and more. It is actually a part of the Microsoft Office 365 suite of applications and is available to users with an Office 365 Education or Enterprise license.

With Microsoft Forms, users can create surveys and quizzes with a different variety of question types, including multiple choice, text, rating, date, and more. Forms can be designed with customizable themes and branding, and can be shared with others via email or a link.

Responses to forms are collected in real-time and can be viewed and analyzed in Microsoft Forms or exported to other applications such as Excel for further analysis. Additionally, Microsoft Forms includes features for collaboration, such as the ability to share forms with others and co-author forms in real-time.

Overall, Microsoft Forms is a versatile tool that can be actually used in a variety of contexts for collecting feedback, assessing knowledge, and gathering information. Its integration with other Microsoft applications makes it a convenient option for users who are already familiar with the Office 365 suite of tools.

Creating and Editing Forms

Creating and editing Microsoft Forms is a straightforward process that can actually be done by anyone with a Microsoft Office 365 Education or Enterprise account. Here are the basic steps:

1. **Open Microsoft Forms:** Go to the Office 365 portal and click on the Forms app to open it.
2. **Create a new form:** Click on the "New Form" button to start creating a new form. Give the form a name and add any additional information such as a description or instructions.
3. **Add questions:** Click on the "Add question" button to add questions to your form. Microsoft Forms offers an actual variety of question types, including multiple choice, text, rating, date, and more. You can also add images or videos to your questions.

4. **Customize your form:** Customize your form by changing the theme, adding your own branding, and adding a background image.

5. **Share your form:** Once your form is complete, you can actually share it with others via email, link, or embed code. You can also set up options for response collection, such as requiring respondents to log in to provide responses.

6. **Review and analyze responses:** As responses come in, you can review and analyze them within Microsoft Forms. You can also export the data to other applications such as Excel for further analysis.

Editing your form is just as easy. Simply open your form, click on the "Edit" button, and make any changes you need to the questions, settings, or design.

Sharing Forms with Others

Sharing Microsoft Forms with others is a great way to get feedback, opinions, or data from a wider audience. Microsoft Forms allows you to share your forms in several ways. Here are some of the methods you can use to share your Microsoft Forms with others:

1. **Share a link:** One of the easiest ways to share your Microsoft Form is to share a link to the form. You can copy the link by clicking on the "Share" button and selecting "Copy". You can then share the link through email, instant messaging, or social media.

2. **Embed the form:** If you have a website or blog, you can embed the form directly into the page. To do this, click on the "Share" button and select "Embed". You can then copy the embed code and paste it into your website or blog.

3. **Share through Microsoft Teams:** If you are working on a project with a team in Microsoft Teams, you can share your Microsoft Form directly in the team's

channel. To do this, click on the "Share" button and select "Teams". You can then select the team and channel you want to share the form with.

4. **Share through OneDrive:** If you have a OneDrive account, you can share your Microsoft Form through OneDrive. To do this, click on the "Share" button and select "OneDrive". You can then select the folder you want to save the form in and share the link to the form.

5. **Share through QR code:** Microsoft Forms also allows you to share your form through a QR code. To do this, click on the "Share" button and select "QR code". You can then save the QR code image and share it with others.

In addition to these methods, you can also restrict access to your Microsoft Form by requiring respondents to sign in with their Microsoft account, or by setting a password for the form.

Collecting and Analyzing Responses

Microsoft Forms provides features to help you collect and analyze responses from surveys, quizzes, and other types of forms. Here are some of the key features for collecting and analyzing responses in Microsoft Forms:

1. **Response collection:** Microsoft Forms enables you to collect responses from a variety of sources, including email invitations, links, and embedded forms. You can also customize the form settings to limit responses to a specific time frame or number of respondents.

2. **Response analysis:** Microsoft Forms provides tools to help you analyze responses, including built-in charts and graphs that visualize response data. You can also filter and sort responses by question, answer, or respondent.

3. **Collaboration and sharing:** Microsoft Forms enables you to share and collaborate on forms and responses with others. You can invite others to collaborate on a form or share a read-only link to view response data.

4. **Integration with other Microsoft tools:** Microsoft Forms can be integrated with other Microsoft tools, such as Excel and Power BI, to provide advanced reporting and analysis capabilities. This enables you to analyze response data in more depth and create custom reports and dashboards.

5. **Exporting responses:** Microsoft Forms allows you to export response data to Excel or other formats for further analysis or reporting. You can also choose to export all responses or only selected responses based on specific criteria.

In summary, Microsoft Forms provides a range of features to help you collect and analyze responses from forms. With built-in response collection and analysis tools, collaboration and sharing capabilities, and integration with other Microsoft tools, you can easily collect and analyze responses to gain insights and make data-driven decisions.

Integrating Forms with other Office 365 Apps

Microsoft Forms can be integrated with other Office 365 apps to provide a more seamless and efficient experience for users. Here are some examples of how Microsoft Forms can integrate with other Office 365 apps:

1. **SharePoint:** Microsoft Forms can be embedded in SharePoint to provide a custom user interface for data entry and data collection. This enables users to interact with forms in a more intuitive and user-friendly way.

2. **Excel:** Microsoft Forms can be integrated with Excel to enable users to access and update Excel data directly from the form. This can be useful for managing data-intensive processes, such as budgeting or financial reporting.

3. **Microsoft Teams:** Microsoft Forms can be integrated with Microsoft Teams to enable team members to access and complete forms directly within the Teams environment. This can help to streamline collaboration and increase productivity.

4. **Power Automate:** Microsoft Forms can be integrated with Power Automate (formerly known as Microsoft Flow) to automate processes and workflows based on form responses. This can help to save time and reduce errors by automating repetitive or manual tasks.

5. **Power Apps:** Microsoft Forms can be integrated with Power Apps to enable users to build custom apps based on form data. This can help to provide a more customized and integrated solution for data collection and analysis.

In summary, integrating Microsoft Forms with other Office 365 apps can help to improve productivity, streamline collaboration, and provide a more seamless user experience. By integrating with SharePoint, Excel, Microsoft Teams, Power Automate, and Power Apps, you can create a powerful and integrated suite of apps that meet your specific business needs.

Power Apps

Microsoft Power Apps is actually a low-code platform that enables users to build custom business applications without writing code. With Power Apps, users can create applications that run on various devices and platforms, including mobile devices, web browsers, and tablets.

The platform provides a wide range of pre-built templates, connectors, and data sources to simplify application development. It also includes a drag-and-drop user interface that makes it easy to build and customize the application's layout and functionality.

Power Apps can integrate with various other Microsoft services such as Microsoft Dynamics 365, Microsoft Power BI, Microsoft Teams, and SharePoint, to help users extend their business processes and increase productivity.

Overall, Power Apps can help organizations and individuals create custom applications tailored to their specific needs, without requiring extensive technical skills or resources.

Introduction to Microsoft Power Apps

Microsoft's Power Apps program enables you to quickly create and distribute robust low-code apps. It is a collection of software, services, and data platforms that enables quick application development to create unique software depending on corporate needs.

If your company data is on-premises (Excel, Office 365, SharePoint, and others), on a data platform (a common data source for applications), or both, you may easily construct bespoke business apps that link to that data.

At its heart, Power Apps is a platform as a service that enables you to develop programs that work with any mobile platform or web browser. To enable users to create apps with additional features without coding knowledge, Power Apps were created. Microsoft boasts that PowerApps have an initial visual design and drag-and-drop capability.

Power Apps provides links to several Microsoft-based and third-party programs, including Google Docs, Dropbox, Dynamics CRM, and Oracle, as well as SharePoint, SQL Server, and OneDrive in the actual Office 365 productivity suite.

The fact that Power Apps may be used by both technical and non-technical teams sets it apart from competing products.

Microsoft PowerApps Features

With the use of Power Apps' capabilities, you may create apps without knowing any code. The impressive features of Power Apps are given below:

- **Easy integration with other Microsoft services:** The fact that Power Apps integrate so well with other Microsoft services like Excel, OneDrive, SharePoint, etc. is one of the main benefits of utilizing them.

- **User-friendly Interface:** An intuitive user interface is supported by Power Apps. Even if you have no prior knowledge with coding, you can still simply create an app with this. Build CRUD-capable interfaces for applications.
- **Canvas Apps and Model-driven Apps:** Power Apps offers two methods for creating apps: Canvas and Model-driven Method. Just dragging and dropping pieces onto a canvas is all it takes to develop an app. With model-driven apps, the components you add dictate and specify a large portion of the layout.
- **Cloud Connectivity:** With Power Apps, connecting to cloud services like SQL, Dropbox, Google Drive, etc. is quite simple.
- **App creation and sharing:** Supports the building of programs using a simple drag-and-drop interface. Power Apps make sharing with whomever you want simple.
- **Cost-effective:** Use this wonderful tool if you want to create robust commercial apps but lack the funds for developers. Power Apps are reasonably priced.
- **Common Data Service (CDS):** You may securely manage and store data used by business apps with CDS. Entities are used to hold data within CDS. An entity is a collection of records that functions like a database table in that it holds data. There are several legal bodies in CDS for Apps that deal with common situations. Custom entities specific to your business may still be established, and they can be filled with data using Power Query. With this data, developers may create sophisticated apps utilizing Power Apps.

Building Custom Business Applications

Microsoft Power Apps is actually a low-code development platform that enables users to create custom business applications quickly and easily, without the need for extensive coding experience. Here are the basic steps for building custom business applications using Power Apps:

1. **Define the app's purpose:** Before building the app, you should define its purpose and scope. Consider the business process or problem the app will address, the data sources and workflows required, and the user experience you want to create.

2. **Choose a template or start from scratch:** Power Apps provides a range of templates to help you get started, including apps for project management, customer service, and inventory management. You can also start from scratch and create a custom app using a blank canvas.

3. **Connect to data sources:** Power Apps allows you to connect to a wide range of data sources, including SharePoint, Dynamics 365, and Excel. You can also create custom connectors to connect to other data sources.

4. **Design the user interface:** Power Apps provides a drag-and-drop interface for designing the app's user interface. You can add screens, forms, galleries, and other controls to create the user experience you want. You can also actually customize the look and feel of the app using themes and styles.

5. **Create workflows and logic:** Power Apps provides a range of built-in functions and formulas for creating workflows and logic within the app. You can also create custom functions using Power Apps' formula language, which is similar to Excel formulas.

6. **Test and deploy the app:** Once you have built the app, you can test it using the built-in preview feature. You can also share the app with other users for testing and feedback. Once the app is ready, you can deploy it to your organization using Power Apps' built-in deployment features.

Integrating with other Office 365 Apps

Microsoft Power Apps can be integrated with other Office 365 apps to provide a more seamless and efficient experience for users. Here are some examples of how Power Apps can integrate with other Office 365 apps:

1. **SharePoint:** Power Apps can be integrated with SharePoint to provide a custom user interface for SharePoint lists and libraries. This enables users to interact with SharePoint data in a more intuitive and user-friendly way.

2. **Excel:** Power Apps can be integrated with Excel to enable users to access and update Excel data directly from the app. This can be useful for managing data-intensive processes, such as budgeting or financial reporting.

3. **Microsoft Teams:** Power Apps can be integrated with Microsoft Teams to enable team members to access and work on the app directly within the Teams environment. This can help to streamline collaboration and increase productivity.

4. **Power Automate:** Power Apps can be integrated with Power Automate (formerly known as Microsoft Flow) to automate processes and workflows within the app. This can help to save time and reduce errors by automating repetitive or manual tasks.

5. **Power BI:** Power Apps can be integrated with Power BI to enable users to create and view interactive reports and dashboards based on the app's data. This can help to provide insights into business performance and inform decision-making.

In summary, integrating Power Apps with other Office 365 apps can help to improve productivity, streamline collaboration, and provide a more seamless user experience. By integrating with SharePoint, Excel, Microsoft Teams, Power Automate, and Power BI, you can create a powerful and integrated suite of apps that meet your specific business needs.

Sharing and Collaborating on Apps

Microsoft Power Apps is actually a powerful platform for building custom business applications without the need for extensive coding experience. Once you have created an app in Power Apps, you can share and collaborate on it with others. Here are actually some of the ways you can share and collaborate on Power Apps:

1. **Sharing an app:** To share an app with others, you can use the "Share" button in the Power Apps studio. You can then invite users or groups to view, edit, or manage the app. You can also set permissions for each user or group, so that they can only view or edit certain parts of the app.

2. **Co-authoring an app:** Co-authoring allows multiple users to work on the same app at the same time. This can be a useful feature for teams who are collaborating on an app. To enable co-authoring, you can click on the "Collaborate" button in the Power Apps studio and add users or groups who will be co-authoring the app. You can also set permissions for each co-author, so that they can only view or edit certain parts of the app.

3. **Sharing data sources:** Power Apps allows you to share data sources with others, so that they can use the same data in their own apps. To share a data source, you can go to the "Data" tab in the Power Apps studio, click on the data source you want to share, and then click on the "Share" button. You can then invite users or groups to access the data source.

4. **Sharing components:** Power Apps allows you to create and share reusable components, such as forms, screens, or controls. To share a component, you can click on the component in the Power Apps studio, click on the "Export" button, and then share the file with others. Other users can then import the component into their own apps.

5. **Integrating with Microsoft Teams:** Power Apps can be integrated with Microsoft Teams, so that team members can access and work on the app directly within the Teams environment. To do this, you can go to the Teams app store, search for Power Apps, and then add the app to your Teams account.

Analyzing App Usage and Performance

Microsoft Power Apps provides built-in analytics and reporting features that enable you to monitor and analyze app usage and performance. Here are some of the key features for analyzing app usage and performance:

1. **Usage analytics:** Power Apps provides usage analytics that allow you to track the number of app launches, unique users, and sessions over time. This can help you understand how your app is being used and identify any usage patterns or trends.

2. **Performance analytics:** Power Apps also provides performance analytics that enable you to track the app's performance metrics, such as response times and data refresh rates. This can help you identify any performance issues and optimize the app's performance.

3. **Custom reporting:** Power Apps allows you to create custom reports and dashboards that actually provide insights into app usage and performance. You can use these reports to identify opportunities for improvement and make data-driven decisions about app development.

4. **Integration with Power BI:** Power Apps can be integrated with Power BI to provide advanced analytics and reporting capabilities. This enables you to create interactive reports and dashboards based on app usage and performance data, and share these insights with stakeholders.

In summary, analyzing app usage and performance is a critical part of app development and maintenance. With Power Apps' built-in analytics and reporting features, you can monitor usage and performance metrics, create custom reports and dashboards, and use data-driven insights to optimize your app's performance and improve the user experience.

Conclusion

Microsoft Office 365 is a powerful suite of productivity tools that can actually help you streamline your workflow, improve collaboration, and increase productivity. Whether you're working on documents, spreadsheets, presentations, or forms, Office 365 provides a range of features and capabilities to help you get your work done more efficiently.

Throughout this guide, we've explored some of the key features and capabilities of Office 365, including Word, Excel, PowerPoint, Forms, and Power Apps. We've also looked at some of the ways in which Office 365 can be integrated with other apps and services to provide a more seamless and integrated experience.

Whether you're a beginner just getting started with Office 365 or an experienced user looking to learn more about the platform, there's always something new to discover and explore. By taking advantage of the actual features and capabilities of Office 365, you can improve your productivity, streamline your workflow, and get more done in less time.

So if you're ready to start using Office 365 to its fullest potential, don't be afraid to dive in and explore all that this powerful platform has to offer. With a very little bit of time and effort, you'll actually be well on your way to becoming an Office 365 power user.

www.ingramcontent.com/pod-product-compliance
Lightning Source LLC
LaVergne TN
LVHW082338200926
848481LV00012B/3382
* 9 7 9 8 8 9 8 4 3 2 2 7 0 *